Real Estate Investment

Theories and Analysis

Bryan Law

Fox College of Business

First edition: April 2021

Fox College of Business

ISBN 978-0-9881217-8-2

Disclaimer

Fox College of Business and Bryan Law are not engaged in rendering legal, accounting, real estate, or other professional services. This book should not be relied upon as providing such advice. We strongly urge that you seek professional advice prior to acting on the information contained herein.

The information contained herein has been obtained from sources which we believe are reliable, but we cannot guarantee its accuracy or completeness. Fox College of Business, Bryan Law, and every person involved in creating this book disclaim any warranty as to the accuracy, completeness, and currency of the contents of this book. We also disclaim all liability in respect of the results of any action taken or not taken in reliance upon information in this book.

Preface

This book helps investors analyze the increasingly sophisticated real estate marketplace by studying properties from different angles, especially from the financial aspects. Simple investment calculations sufficed in the past, but investors in today's real estate market must perform complex comparisons to get the best analyses for their investments.

Real estate professionals always emphasize the importance of the location of a property. Therefore, it is crucial to talk about real estate planning and development theories in this book.

Financial professionals use the present value of future earnings as the benchmark for analyzing returns. Therefore, this book focuses on the estimation, analysis and comparison of cash flows and returns so that buyers and sellers can carefully study alternatives and make informed decisions.

This book provides investors and analysts with reliable tools to make sound decisions while acknowledging that solving individual situations requires flexibility and creativity.

Bryan Law BSc (Pure Maths), LLM, LLD

A well-known author, consultant, and educator in Canada, Bryan has a diversified professional background.

Bryan is a management consultant with more than 20 years of experience. He is also a legal researcher in various areas, including contract law, environmental law, human rights law, labour law, privacy law, and real estate law.

Different education institutions have hired Bryan to provide his expertise in business management, law, and real estate. Bryan has authored over 20 books in various disciplines, including human rights, creative problem-solving, franchising, real estate, Feng Shui, employment law, and more.

Bryan's wide-ranging knowledge and professional experience, coupled with humorous presentation skills, have placed him in demand as a professional speaker as well.

Table of Contents

1: Introduction

Real estate may be the oldest kind of investment tool in human history. The value of the real estate, such as farmlands, will appreciate over time. Real estate investment started with leasing out farmlands and homes. Different kinds of investment properties have been developed in modern societies, such as condominium office buildings and retirement housings.

How to judge the value of a piece of land was a relatively simple task in rural societies in the past, as the sole purpose was to use it as farmland. Whether the earth structure was sand-based, rock-based, clay-based or soil-based might be the only criteria to determine its value. As the societies evolved, farmlands can be invested to rent out to peasants and develop them into real properties for different uses. A more quantitative or objective method to evaluate lands is required.

Through the years, analysts and investors have developed different systems to analyze real properties using proven techniques and reliable investment methodologies and theories. Although those techniques, methods and approaches can also be used in residential real estate, they are instrumental in analyzing commercial real estate. More correctly, those analyses are used to evaluate income-generating properties and are based on financial models.

Since financial analyses rely on the current or future cash flow produced by the properties, such analyses cannot be applied to real properties with no actual or projected rental income. For example, a piece of vacant land with no rental income may still be a good investment for its development potential and should be evaluated using different approaches. Therefore, the first analysis in this book will focus on geographic analysis, while the rest will be different types of financial analyses.

Geographic Analysis

Size can be measured, but not everything can be measured or can be measured objectively. For example, the qualities of two retail units of the same size in the same shopping mall cannot be measured directly. They can only be analyzed and assigned a value with different criteria. Two development lots of the same size have a similar situation. Suppose both of them are ten acres in size. In that case, the price per acre cannot be calculated objectively as the two lots are in different locations and may be subject to different zoning use too.

Location, location, location! That is not just a mantra used in the real estate field about real estate values; it is one of the most critical factors that would affect the value of a property. Location is essential when it comes to the value of a property. On the other hand, although there are some basic principles to follow, it is not possible to measure the value of a site without some subjective estimation.

Geographic analysis is a vital tool to study certain areas such as business intelligence, housing development, retail location, and urban growth. Overall, it helps appraisers and analysts to estimate the potential of a property or a site.

Although this book focuses on the financial analyses of real properties with different approaches, it will also address key value concepts and value principles that are fundamental in assessing the values of real properties, especially their potential to develop and grow in value. The concepts of value, theories in urban economics and principles used in the valuation process will be discussed in the following chapters.

Mortgage Financing

A loan can be an ongoing credit line that does not require the borrower to pay off the debt. In fact, a lender wants their clients to maintain the loan balance so that they will continually pay the interest. To the lender, it is a business with indefinitely cash flow.

A mortgage for real estate is not the same. A mortgage must be amortized over a period of time so that the borrower will pay off the debt at the end of that period. Amortization is the gradual retirement of a debt by means of periodic mortgage payments that consist of partial principal and interest. Under this arrangement, the lender advances the mortgage loan to the borrower on the completion date of the real estate purchase, which is then repaid by that borrower through subsequent payments as determined by an amortization schedule.

The length of amortization affects how long the mortgage will be paid off and the amount of mortgage payment for each period. The payment period can be monthly, biweekly or weekly, with some minor variations. Each mortgage payment within an amortized mortgage is called a blended payment, as it includes both payments towards the principal and interest. While a loan payment can be used to pay only the interest, a mortgage payment will be the interest amount plus a principal payment to pay down the balance.

In some jurisdictions, such as Canada, the interest of a mortgage loan is only allowed to be calculated twice a year, not in advance, as the maximum. However, the payment frequency is at least 12 times a year (monthly payment). There is a need to adjust the interest calculations from semi-annual to monthly to match the payment frequency. We will discuss the details in Chapter 5.

Financial Analysis

Some say mathematics has only black and white, so it is easy to make judgments. Numbers are indeed objective measures of qualities. Therefore, financial analyses are used as an objective measure to estimate the values of real properties, and we can compare properties in different locations without judging them subjectively, such as their direction, shapes and colours.

Investors rely on fundamental ratios to compare properties before further investigations to make investment decisions. Fundamental ratios are the rules of thumb; they are simple to use and can provide a rough estimation of the return rate.

A few popular fundamental ratios will be discussed later to offer a clear understanding of both the strengths and weaknesses of those popular estimation methods. Although they are relatively simple, those rules of thumb are essential basic comparison tools. The rules of thumb are usually for convenience rather than confidence. When financial information is limited, their convenience will be appreciated.

Lack of data is often a major obstacle, preventing analysts from seeking detailed financial analysis and hindering negotiations between buyers and sellers.

The time value of money is the crucial concept in all complex financial analyses. The methods of compounding and discounting represent the necessary skills to determine the time value of money. The calculations involve the variables Present Value (PV), Rate per Period (I/YR), Number of Periods per Year (N), Payment per Period (PMT) and Future Value (FV).

Compounding is the amount by which an investment will grow over a given number of time periods, including both the principal amount and the accumulation of interest. Discounting is the opposite of compounding. While the principal amount for compounding can be added at each period, discounting may also involve several payments in different periods in the future. That is, discounting is a process of converting future payments into present value. Therefore, discounting fits the situations of real estate investments where rental payments are received each month in the future.

Compounding is often used in investment tools like interest-bearing bank accounts, term deposits, and mutual funds. Simple compounding is less frequently used than discounting in real estate investment analysis since the income generated from a property is not based on the capital invested in the property. It is based on the projected rents receivable in the future.

Before-Tax and After-Tax

A detailed analysis will cover both cash flows before-tax and cash flows after-tax. That can give the investors a clear picture of how the real estate investment would affect their before- and after-tax income, taking income from other investments into consideration. Income from other investments may affect an investor's overall tax rate, especially individual investors.

However, the after-tax calculations will not be discussed in this book since the rates and calculation methods vary from investor to investor and from jurisdiction to jurisdiction.

2. Urban Economics

Many factors may affect the desirability of one property over another, including its features and benefits. Those are often subjective measures. Cities are developed from villages and townships when people settle scattered before well-planned strategies are established to regulate the development of lands. Land use has also expanded from mainly residential and agricultural to retail, office, industrial, and more. In order to study how to plan the land use and valuate real properties, urban economics and different value principles were developed to help the real estate professionals.

Urban Economics

Urban economics is a mix of economics and geography. Economics focuses on how individuals and societies allocate scarce resources to meet their needs and desires, while geography is studying the earth, its spatial characteristics and its impact on human activities. Urban economics goes beyond the interaction between geographic supply and demand and human activities to cover a broader range of issues.

It studies how cities should be developed, how various forces affect land use in towns and regions, how these factors affect location decisions and the impact of such decisions on current and future urban planning.

Different theories are used to examine how a city or town is developed or should be developed according to the structure of an urban environment, such as business and industrial developments, transportation systems, and the distribution of residential zones.

Concentric Circle Model

The Concentric Zone Model, also known as the Burgess model, is one of the earliest models to explain urban social structures. It was proposed by Ernest Burgess, an urban sociologist from the University of Chicago, in 1925.

It describes urban growth in terms of concentric circles spreading out from a central business core, which contains five zones:

1. Central Business District
2. Transition and Factory Zone
3. Working Class Homes
4. Middle and Higher Income Homes
5. Suburban and Commuter Zone

Figure 1 below illustrates the concept of the Concentric Circle Model.

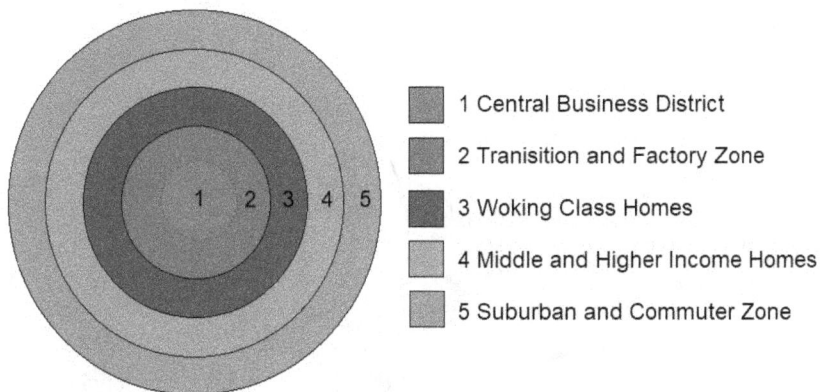

1 Central Business District

2 Tranisition and Factory Zone

3 Woking Class Homes

4 Middle and Higher Income Homes

5 Suburban and Commuter Zone

Figure 1

Axial Model

After Burgess proposed his Concentric Model, it has been challenged by many urban geographers. The advancement in transportation and information technology makes city planning impossible to be organized with clearly defined zones or simplified zoning use.

Some geographers and theorists have built models such as the Axial Model for that reason. Axis model includes commuting time as a factor in urban development, based on the Concentric Circle Model and transportation system allowance composition. The more efficient the transportation system, the greater the growth that will occur along that route.

Figure 2 below illustrates the concept of the Axial Model.

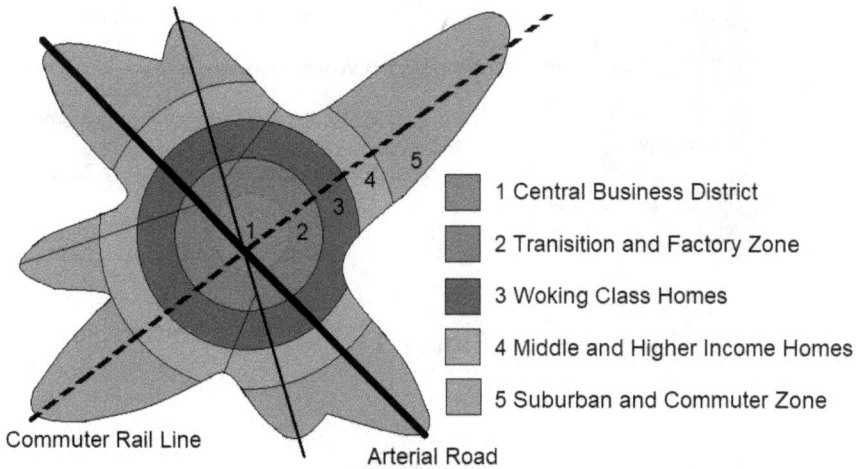

1 Central Business District

2 Tranisition and Factory Zone

3 Woking Class Homes

4 Middle and Higher Income Homes

5 Suburban and Commuter Zone

Commuter Rail Line

Arterial Road

Figure 2

Sector Model

Another urban economist Homer Hoyt introduced the Sector Model in 1941. He pointed out that due to transportation and other factors, development trends are flowing out of the central business district. Commercial areas are located near busy roads, middle-income residential regions are developed in preferred but not optimal locations, and more impoverished areas occupied less desirable areas adjacent to railroads. The outward growth of each sector is divided by factors such as income and social class, as opposed to a homogenous group assumed by Burgess.

Figure 3 below illustrates the concept of the Sector Model.

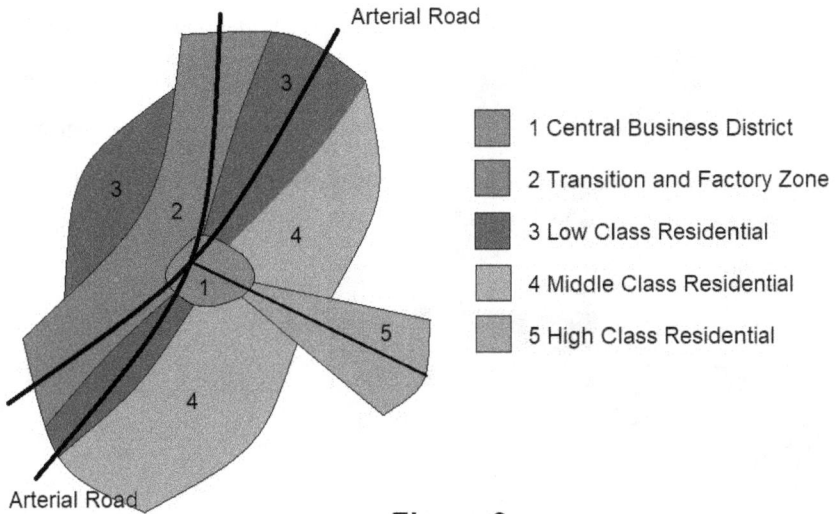

Figure 3

Legend:
1 Central Business District
2 Transition and Factory Zone
3 Low Class Residential
4 Middle Class Residential
5 High Class Residential

Multiple Nuclei Model

Subsequent urban economists further refine the above three models by moving away from a standalone central business district to address the growth of suburban core commercial areas. Instead of using one central business district as the centre for urban development to emanate, multiple centres are used in the Multiple Nuclei Model. Most modern cities usually have the components of all the above three models. However, the Multiple Nuclei Model is best suited for metropolitans.

Figure 4 below illustrates the concept of the Multiple Nuclei Model.

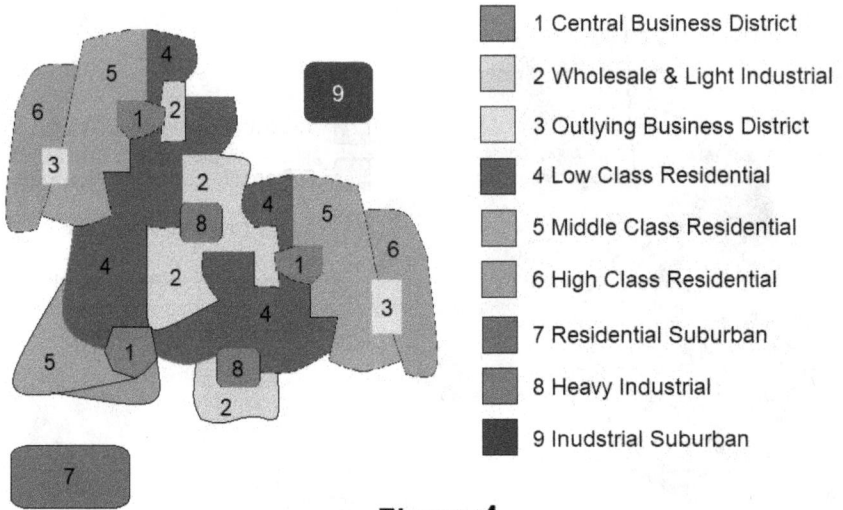

	1 Central Business District
	2 Wholesale & Light Industrial
	3 Outlying Business District
	4 Low Class Residential
	5 Middle Class Residential
	6 High Class Residential
	7 Residential Suburban
	8 Heavy Industrial
	9 Inudstrial Suburban

Figure 4

Trends and Real Estate Values

Although not all municipals will use the above models to plan their urban developments, those models provide the basic ideas of how a city will naturally develop into different zones according to different income, social, business, and use groups. City planners and real estate investors should know how one particular zone will impact the developments of its neighbouring vacant lands.

Knowing those models, or the ones that the planning department uses, is crucial in performing real estate development. One must understand how a municipality will develop its land before developing a new subdivision, buying a property next to a piece of vacant land, or with raw lands nearby.

Once the planning model is known, and a site is picked as a development target, the next step is to estimate the value of the site and the projected value of the building after it is developed. All kinds of estimations have to be based on the market data obtained from the land registry offices or local real estate boards. However, sometimes it is also necessary to rely on hearsay evidence.

Because market conditions, including economic, social and political factors, change rapidly, the estimation or projection may only be valid for a short period of time. Land development also involves the study of planning and the highest and best use of that piece of land, but such discussions go beyond the scope of this text.

Urban Density and Infill

While the developments of new subdivisions rely on the city planning of that municipality, a developed neighbourhood may still have development potential for intensification. Increasing urban density through effective urban redevelopment is an excellent way to provide more inventory to the real estate market.

When there are no vacant lands in the neighbourhood for development sites, increasing urban density is required. Such urban intensification includes expanding the use of buildings and serviced land to provide additional real estate stock and more effectively utilize existing municipal services instead of creating new properties through outlying subdivision developments. In residential, it refers to infill.

In urban planning, infill refers to any project that creates new housing within an existing, established neighbourhood. It includes the demolition of an existing structure with a low density, with its replacement being a high-density building. For example, developers may take down a few single-family detached homes and construct a high-rise condominium apartment building or build significant additions to existing housing stock to supply more dwelling units.

When dealing with redevelopment, the built form of the neighbourhood has to be considered too. Built form refers to the shape, height, appearance, building materials used and internal configuration within a particular area. For example, the built form of a financial district may be rectangular high-rise buildings with big foyer and glass curtain walls because most of the buildings are for office use. In contrast, the built form of a cottage county may be small detached homes with fireplaces and brick exterior finishes. In addition to the existing densities, property uses, and zoning requirements, municipalities will also take built form into consideration as part of the official planning process.

Demographics

Demography is the statistical study of populations and is a significant factor impacting the real estate market. The first critical demographic factor that will profoundly impact the real estate market is population size and growth. In many countries, immigration is another way to drive a country's population growth in addition to the natural growth rate. The same applies to a municipality or a neighbourhood.

A positive net migration may be the most significant ongoing factor in population growth. For demographic purposes, net migration is the difference between the number of people entering versus the number of people exiting from the area within a specified period of time.

An increase in population will definitely increase the demand for real estate stock. However, even there is no increase in the number of people in a particular neighbourhood, the demand for housing units may also be increased.

For example, there are two families, and a child from each family marries, their marriage sets up a third family. Usually, the new couple would establish an independent household and would look for another housing unit. That is known as the family formation rate. An increase in family formations typically creates a similar increase in demand for housing units.

Population Composition

We can see that the demand for housing units can be increased without any change in the population from the example above. If there are more residents in a particular neighbourhood in the age of 20 to 40, it has a higher possibility that those people will get married or plan to have children soon. Therefore, the need for more housing units in that neighbourhood will possibly be higher.

On the other hand, if the neighbourhood has gradual ageing of the population and more and more people will be 60 or older, such a shift to a more ageing population will bring new demands for senior living style in real estate—properties such as life lease units, retirement homes, supportive and extended care facilities will be in need.

With improved people's overall health, the ageing population is not focused entirely on traditional retirement living styles. As the baby boomers are more active than previous generations, more seniors choose condominium units or bungalows as their "retirement homes". In particular, downtown condominium units are the most attractive choice because most retirees seek the convenience of living in urban centres. Moreover, retirement for many people means there is a need to scale down house size. Condominium complexes provide a lifestyle choice to seniors that are easy to manage, complete with recreational and social amenities, and some with support services.

Population Distribution

In terms of real estate development, population growth within a country may not favour all cities or urban areas. Similarly, the population growth within a municipality may not favour all neighbourhoods in that municipality. The increase in population may result from a net natural birth rate, more new immigrants to that country, or a positive net migration in the region. Net migration is usually caused by an increase in employment opportunities in that region. Therefore, a Location Quotient (LQ) should be calculated to better analyze the real estate market due to that increase.

The term Location Quotient quantifies how concentrated a particular industry or occupation is in a region compared to the national average. It is a simple ratio and can also be used to compare other economic measures or demographic groups. For example, the aircraft manufacturing industry employs 100,000 people in a municipality, equivalent to 3% of the workforce. If the national average of employment in aircraft manufacturing is only 0.5% of the workforce, then the LQ is 3% ÷ 0.5%, which is 6.0.

An LQ above 1.3 usually indicates a high degree of concentration in that particular industry within that municipality. The number of employees in that industry is also a crucial factor to decide its impact on that municipality's employment and economy. If both the LQ and number of employees are high, any inside or outside changes in that industry will affect that municipality's employment, economy and housing market.

In the above example, if an aircraft manufacturing company relocates their factory from that municipality to another city, many workers may lose their jobs or have to relocate with the factory to the other city. That will impact the real estate market in both municipalities. The city where the new factory is located will have a significant increase in net migration. The LQ distribution is an essential piece of information in studying the development potential of a particular municipality.

Environmental Concerns

Many real estate development plans are subject to environmental protection restrictions. More and more municipalities are introducing stricter zoning provisions to improve environmental protection and proper planning. Suppose a portion of the development land falls within an environmental zone. In that case, additional restrictions will apply to the building setbacks, location of a building on that land and total building and parking coverage.

To apply for a change in land use, the applicant may have to provide studies on sewage capacity in serviced areas, stormwater management, the impact on existing municipal infrastructure, site noise on adjacent areas, and the impact on the environment. For industrial and commercial properties, environmental contamination and hazardous waste are the primary concerns of vacant lands and existing buildings. Therefore, environmental assessment is one of the required procedures in due diligence before buying any industrial and commercial properties, as hazards and contamination can represent a significant risk and adversely affect the value of the property.

3. Value Principles

Value is defined as a fair return or equivalent in goods, services, or money for something exchanged. In real estate and most fields, money is used to measure the values. However, the meaning and calculation of value are not unique, and the term value has many definitions as there are different types of value. For example, a municipality tax officer usually thinks of property value in terms of assessed value. An insurance company thinks of replacement value, an accountant thinks of book value, and an appraiser thinks of market value. It is, therefore, crucial to understand the different meanings of value.

Objective Value and Subjective Value

Before knowing the principles used to determine values, we have to know the definition of value first. Value is best described as the goods, services, or money of one thing that can be obtained in exchange for another, and money is commonly used to measure the value of the real estate. Value can be subjective and objective. A subjective value exists in the mind of the buyer or seller, while an objective value is often tied to the cost of reproduction. In real estate, buyers and sellers negotiate based on the subjective value in their minds. However, the final sale price is often the objective value based on the market performance and comparable properties. For an investment property, financial data of that property is also used.

Value in Exchange and Value in Use

The concept of the difference between the value in exchange and the value in use is an interesting one, which often affects the decision of sellers when deciding the sale price. Value in exchange is defined as the probable price at which one thing trades in a free, competitive and open market. Value in use is the value attributed to an item by the owner who is using that item. For example, an old, low-end and rusting car may have no value in the used car market, so its value in exchange is zero. However, the old car owner relies on it for commuting to work, so it has some value in use to the owner. If the lowest price of a used car in the market is $500, then the value in use of that old car can be estimated as $500 to the owner.

Market Price and Market Value

Another concept in valuation is the difference between market price and market value. Simply speaking, the market price of a property is the price that the buyer paid for that property. In contrast, the market value is the estimate of value using market data such as the market prices of similar properties, the market expected rate of return, or the market prices of material and labour to reproduce the property.

The market price of a property is fixed, as it is the price paid by the buyer. However, its market value may vary, and different people may have different opinions on it. Market value is, in fact, the value in exchange to be determined. In real estate, the definitions of market value vary, depending on what type of property is being appraised and the use to which the appraisal is to be put.

A well-accepted definition of market value is:

The most probable price, as of a specified date, in cash or cash-equivalent price for which the specified property would change hands after reasonable exposure in a competitive market under all conditions requisite to a fair sale, with the buyer and seller each acting prudently, knowledgeably and for self-interest, and assuming that neither being compelled to buy or sell.

The above definition emphasizes the exposure in a competitive market; both buyer and seller are well-informed and not under pressure. Moreover, the market value of a property is only an estimate of its price, which is the most probable price on a specified date.

Investment Value

The concept of investment value differs from the concept of market value. Market value is more objective in a way that it is the same to every buyer and seller, but investment value is unique to the investor, either the buyer or seller. Investment value is defined as the value of an investment property from the perspective of a specific investor. Since buyers and sellers have their unique circumstances, that can affect yield and the valuation estimate.

For example, an investor's marginal tax rate, which varies among investors, may affect after-tax income projections, impacting the after-tax income flows and how a buyer will offer a market value to buy the property. In other words, the rationale of investment value equals roughly the rationale of the value in use discussed above.

Principles of Value

Principle of Anticipation

Under the principle of anticipation, value is created by anticipating the property's benefits, either money to be derived or amenities to be enjoyed in the future. We look for the present value of all future benefits. When buying a home, buyers anticipate that certain benefits will accrue in the coming years, and the purchase price is based on the present worth of those anticipated benefits. When buying an investment property, buyers anticipate that the net income will accrue and increase in the coming years, and the purchase price is based on the present value of those future incomes.

Principle of Balance

Under the principle of balance, the value of a property depends on the balance of land, labour, capital and entrepreneurship in a particular market. A region with an ample supply of land may not be able to maintain the high value of real properties. A city that lacks labour may cause inflation in new construction costs. A market that lacks capital may not be able to do any real estate development. A real estate market that lacks entrepreneurship means there are fewer investors to buy real properties.

Principle of Change

Under the principle of change, the changes in the economic and social environment will affect the value of real properties. Basically, the principle indicates real estate has a cycle of four stages similar to the economic one. The four stages are expansion, peak, contraction and trough. The current cycle can be stable or change in a short period right after the appraisal is done. That is why all appraisers will have to forecast if there would be a change in the market trend within a short period and state such possibility in the report with their justification and assumptions. The appraiser will have to state the effective date of the appraisal in the report as well.

Principle of Competition

Under the principle of competition, the value of a property will be adversely affected by having similar properties in the market for sale as competitors, as buyers have more choices and may not offer a high price to get the property. However, the value may go up if the competition is among buyers. When there are two or more offers on the same property, the buyers may need to offer a higher price to get that property.

Principle of Conformity

Under the principle of conformity, the maximum value of a property is realized when it is utilized to reasonably conform with the existing standards of the area. The highest and best use of the land can also be realized under circumstances of conformity or harmony. Conformity refers to not only the neighbourhood, such as the built form, but also all zoning regulations and private deed restrictions.

Principle of Consistent Use

Under the principle of consistent use, a property must be valued based on a use that is consistent with the property's highest and best use. As a result, land and improvements must be valued on the same basis. For example, suppose an appraiser is estimating the market value of a big lot improved with an old detached house and estimates that the highest and best use is for a retail plaza development. In that case, the appraisal should not accord any value to the detached house over the land.

Principle of Contribution

Under the principle of contribution, also known as the principle of marginal productivity, the value of any property component is measured by how much it adds to the market value of the property rather than as a separate component. A fireplace, a double car garage and a finished basement have their own contribution to the value of a house. The cost of a component does not necessarily equal its contributory value. For investment properties, the value of the components is measured by how much it adds to the overall net income of that property.

Principle of External Factors

Under the principle of external factors, the value of a property can be affected by circumstances and situations near the property, including nearby neighbours and more distant locations. For example, suppose a major bank moves its head office to a neighbourhood in a city. The values of all properties in the same city may increase as the move of the bank's head office resulting in a significant number of new jobs. That will increase the demand for properties. On the other hand, suppose there is an airport in a city, then the values of those real properties near the airport will be affected adversely by the airport due to the high noise level produced by the aeroplanes.

Principle of Highest and Best Use

Under the principle of highest and best use, the value of a property is appraised as though it were being put to its most profitable use, given probable legal, physical, and financial constraints. Such use, either existing use or proposed use, must be allowed by the government. It must fit the size, shape, topography, and other specific characteristics associated with the location. There must be a demand for such use in the market for resale or the use will generate and sustain sufficient income to cover construction costs.

Principle of Increasing and Decreasing Returns

Under the principle of increasing and decreasing returns, also known as the principle of diminishing returns, an increase in components, benefits, or amenities may produce increased returns, up to the point of a maximum return (the point of diminishing returns). After that limit, any increase in those items will not produce a return commensurate with the additional expenditures.

Suppose a detached single-car garage may increase the value of a house by $80,000 while its cost is only $60,000. When we build two such garages, the value increases by $140,000. However, when we build three garages, the value increases by only $170,000, but the cost is $180,000. The increase in the number of garages will increase the net value until there are too many.

Principle of Progression

Under the principle of progression, the value of inferior properties will be affected positively by the presence of the properties of higher value in the same neighbourhood. Suppose there is an old and small bungalow in a community; its value is estimated to be $400,000, then the appraiser does not take the neighbouring houses into consideration. However, since all the homes next to it are two-storey houses and are sold for more than $800,000, the appraiser adjusts the value of the bungalow to $500,000.

Principle of Regression

Under the principle of regression, the value of superior properties will be affected adversely by the presence of the properties of lower value in the same neighbourhood. The rationale of this principle is the same as the principle of progression but is in the opposite direction.

Both the principle of progression and the principle of regression are extensions of the principle of conformity and the principle of external factors. The value of a property is affected by the neighbouring properties, which are the external factors, and the subject property has to reasonably conform with the existing standards of the area for its maximum value.

Principle of Substitution

Under the principle of substitution, the value of a property has an upper limit, which is the cost of acquiring an equally desirable substitute, provided that there is no untimely delay. A prudent buyer would pay no more for an income-generating property than it would cost to build or purchase another property that would produce the same income level.

The principle of substitution is closely related to the economic concept of opportunity cost. It presumes that buyers will consider the alternative properties available to them. They will act rationally based on those alternatives and that the substitute property can be acquired without unreasonable delay.

Principle of Supply and Demand

Under the principle of supply and demand, the value of a property is determined by the interaction of the supply of and demand for similar properties as of the date of the evaluation. Buyers and sellers tend to set the price of a property based on the supply of and the demand for similar properties.

If the supply reduces but the demand remains constant, prices will increase. If the demand diminishes, but the supply remains constant, prices will decrease. If both supply and demand increase or decrease proportionately at the same time, prices will remain relatively stable.

Principle of Surplus Productivity

Under the principle of surplus productivity, the value of land with an income-generating property is based on the net income remaining after all expenses necessary to the operation have been paid, and the capital invested in improvements has been satisfied. For example, a property is sold for $1,200,000, which generates a net operating income (NOI) of $180,000.

Based on a return rate of 10% plus a recapture rate of 2.5%, the income earned by the building is $1,200,000 x 12.5% = $150,000. There is $30,000 leftover from the NOI ($180,000 - $150,000), which is the net income earned by the land. Based on the 10% return rate, the land value is $300,000 ($30,000 ÷ 10%). Concepts on return rates will be discussed in the following chapters.

4. Simple Estimations

Real estate investors will do their capital budgeting to analyze and determine which property is worth the funding of cash. The most common term used is Return on Investment (ROI). It is a ratio between the net income earned and investment, often presented in percentage. The net income earned can be the cash flow over a period of time (usually one year) or the net sale proceeds after the sale of the property.

A variety of investment analysis tools such as payback period, cash on cash, discounted cash flow, present value and internal rate of return are used to compare the return of investment of different properties. We will discuss them one by one in the following chapters.

Rules of Thumb

For easy to learn and apply, some simple methods are developed to estimate the rate of return on investment. Those methods are commonly used in the field to give a quick estimate of the value or potential of income-generating properties, including Gross Rent Multiplier, Break-even Ratio, Overall Capitalization Rate, Payback Period and Cash-on-Cash.

All those methods use the before-tax income to analyze the performance of a property; therefore, they are relatively simple and require less background information from the investors. However, all of them will analyze only one-year income, and one of them relies on gross income, which cannot reflect the actual cash flow generated by the property. Moreover, studying before-tax income have limitations and may not fit the situation of a particular investor.

Cash Flow Analysis – Operating Data

Property Name: _____

Down Payment: _____

+ Costs of Acquisition: _____

= Investment at Purchase: _____ + Debt: _____ = Acquisition Price _____

	Mortgage Data	Beginning Balance	Term / Amortization	Number of payments per year	Interest Rate	Payment	Annual Debt Service	Remarks
1.	1st Mortgage							
2.	2nd Mortgage							

Ownership Analysis of Property Income   **Taxable Income**

		Year 1	Year 2	Year 3	Year 4	Year 5
3	Potential Rental Income					
4	Minus: Vacancy & Credit Losses:					
5	Equals: Effective Rental Income					
6	Plus: Other Income					
7	Equals: Gross Operating Income					
8	Minus: Operating Expenses					
9	Equals: Net Operating Income (NOI)					
10	Minus: Non-operating Expense					
11	Minus: Interest - 1st Mortgage					
12	Minus: Interest - 2nd Mortgage					
13	Minus: Amortization of Loan Fees					
14	Minus: Others					
15	Minus: Others					
16	Equals: Subtotal Taxable Income Before Depreciation					
17	Minus: Allowable Depreciation					
18	Equals: Real Estate Taxable Income					
19	Times: Marginal Tax Rate					
20	Equals: Tax Liability on Real Estate Operations					

Cash Flows

21	Net Operating Income					
22	Minus: Annual Debt Service (ADS)					
23	Equals: Cash Flow Before Taxes					
24	Minus: Tax Liability (Line 20)					
25	**Equals Cash Flows After Tax**					

It does not matter what types of methods to use; the financial data of the property must be available for analysis. The Cash Flow Analysis worksheet above shows a typical form used in the field for collecting financial information. Not all of the blanks in the worksheet have to be filled; we will use it to calculate different rates in the following sections and chapters.

Gross Rent Multiplier

By its name, Gross Rent Multiplier (GRM) uses the gross rental income of an investment property for analysis. The gross rental income is used to compare with the price of the property. It is a ratio used to compare different properties to tell which one will get a higher gross income. The formula of it is simple. As the name is Gross Rent Multiplier, it is used to multiply the gross rent of a property to estimate its value. That is,

Value = Gross Rent Multiplier x Gross Rent

In other words, the Gross Rent Multiplier of a property can be obtained by dividing its value (or price) by the gross rent generated.

Gross Rent Multiplier = Value ÷ Gross Rent

For example, an investment building is sold for $1,100,000 with $50,000 acquisition cost and $185,000 annual gross rental income. Its GRM is $1,150,000 ÷ $185,000, = 6.2162.

If a Cash Flow Analysis worksheet is used, it will appear like this:

Cash Flow Analysis – Operating Data

Property Name: 123 Main Street, Main City

Down Payment: $1,100,000

+ Costs of Acquisition: $50,000

= Investment at Purchase: $1,150,000   + Debt: $0   = Acquisition Price $1,150,000

	Mortgage Data	Beginning Balance	Term / Amortization	Number of payments per year	Interest Rate	Payment	Annual Debt Service	Remarks
1.	1st Mortgage							
2.	2nd Mortgage							

Ownership Analysis of Property Income   Taxable Income

		Year 1	Year 2	Year 3	Year 4	Year 5
3	Potential Rental Income	$185,000				
4	Minus: Vacancy & Credit Losses:					
5	Equals: Effective Rental Income					
6	Plus: Other Income					
7	Equals: Gross Operating Income					
8	Minus: Operating Expenses					
9	Equals: Net Operating Income					
10	Minus: Non-operating Expense					
11	Minus: Interest - 1st Mortgage					
12	Minus: Interest - 2nd Mortgage					
13	Minus: Amortization of Loan Fees					
14	Minus: Others					
15	Minus: Others					
16	Equals: Subtotal Taxable Income Before Depreciation					
17	Minus: Allowable Depreciation					
18	Equals: Real Estate Taxable Income					
19	Times: Marginal Tax Rate					
20	Equals: Tax Liability on Real Estate Operations					

Cash Flows

21	Net Operating Income					
22	Minus: Annual Debt Service					
23	Equals: Cash Flow Before Taxes					
24	Minus: Tax Liability (Line 20)					
25	Equals Cash Flows After Tax					

The above examples use potential rental income rather than gross operating income as sometimes there will be a lack of appropriate data. For example, there may be no market information regarding allowances for vacancy and credit losses, or other income is believed to be overestimated. When comparing the GRM, it is crucial to know which type of gross income is used in the market.

Calculations using gross data are only rough estimations, as the gross data does not accurately reflect the actual situation. A corporation may have over one billion dollars of gross profit, but its net profit may be negative. That is, it is losing money. Based on the gross income to estimate the value of a property or a business is risky. However, it is simple and easy.

If you ask the owner of a corporation how much net profit the corporation earned last year, the owner will be reluctant to tell, especially if the corporation is losing money. However, if you ask the owner how much was the gross profit last year, most people will be willing to tell. By the same token, it is much easier to ask for the gross rent figure of a property than asking for the net rent. Therefore, we use Gross Rent Multiplier but not 'Net Rent Multiplier'. GRM can be a monthly ratio, but most people use yearly figures.

Break-even Ratio

A high gross income does not mean that the property can generate enough net income for the investor. Actually, the property may be losing money. So, first of all, investors want to know when a property can break even; or when it will start losing money. The Break-even Ratio is used to tell the risk. Although the net income is not used, Break-even Ratio takes operating income and debt service (annual mortgage payment) into consideration. The formula is:

Break-even Ratio = (Operating Expenses + Debt Service) ÷ Gross Operating Income

Unlike Gross Rent Multiplier, Break-even Ratio does not use potential rental income and must use Gross Operating Income in the calculation. All kinds of operating expenses are taken into consideration, including realty taxes and debt service, but not the profit tax payable. A Break-even Ratio of less than one indicates that the property has a positive cash flow and could tolerate a proportionate decrease in gross operating income or an increase in expenses.

Generally, investors will avoid properties with a Break-even Ratio close to one. A Break-even Ratio that is greater than one means the property is losing money. However, some investors may accept a Break-even Ratio that exceeds one if they believe capital appreciation will appear soon and they will only hold it for a short period. That is more common during a period of high inflation and rising costs.

Let us continue with the example in the GRM calculation above. Suppose the investor applied a mortgage for $600,000, with an interest rate of 5% per year, amortized over 25 years. The monthly mortgage payment is $3,489.63, and the yearly payment is $41,875.56. The Vacancy and

Credit Losses are 5% of the Potential Rental Income, which is $9,250, making the Effective Rental Income $175,750. There is an extra income of $1,250 from the coin laundry machines, so the Gross Operating Income is $177,000. The Operating Expenses are $82,000 per year. As shown in the worksheet below:

Cash Flow Analysis – Operating Data

Property Name: 123 Main Street, Main City

Down Payment: $500,000

+ Costs of Acquisition: $50,000

= Investment at Purchase: $550,000   + Debt: $600,000   = Acquisition Price $1,150,000

	Mortgage Data	Beginning Balance	Term / Amortization	Number of payments per year	Interest Rate	Payment	Annual Debt Service	Remarks
1.	1st Mortgage	$600,000	5 YR/25 YR	12	5%	$3,489.63	$41,875.56	
2.	2nd Mortgage							

Ownership Analysis of Property Income   **Taxable Income**

		Year 1	Year 2	Year 3	Year 4	Year 5
3	Potential Rental Income	$185,000				
4	Minus: Vacancy & Credit Losses:	$9,250				
5	Equals: Effective Rental Income	$175,750				
6	Plus: Other Income	$1,250				
7	Equals: Gross Operating Income	$177,000				
8	Minus: Operating Expenses	$82,000				
9	Equals: Net Operating Income					
10	Minus: Non-operating Expense					
11	Minus: Interest - 1st Mortgage					
12	Minus: Interest - 2nd Mortgage					
13	Minus: Amortization of Loan Fees					
14	Minus: Others					
15	Minus: Others					
16	Equals: Subtotal Taxable Income Before Depreciation					
17	Minus: Allowable Depreciation					
18	Equals: Real Estate Taxable Income					
19	Times: Marginal Tax Rate					
20	Equals: Tax Liability on Real Estate Operations					

Cash Flows

21	Net Operating Income					
22	Minus: Annual Debt Service					
23	Equals: Cash Flow Before Taxes					
24	Minus: Tax Liability (Line 20)					
25	**Equals Cash Flows After Tax**					

Break-Even Ratio = (Operating Expenses + Debt Service)
÷ Gross Operating Income

= ($82,000 + $41,875.56) ÷ $177,000

= 0.7 (70%)

When the Break-Even Ratio of a property is 70%, it means that the property can still be break-even when its gross operating income reduces by 30% or when the sum of its operating expenses and debt service increase by 42.86%.

Overall Capitalization Rate (OCR)

Capitalization is the process of converting net operating income into an indication of value. There are several variations in the capitalization rate. The most straightforward one is calculating the ratio between the net operating income produced by a property and the price paid for the property (or the market value of it). Since both the land and building are group together as a whole in the calculation, this simple version of the capitalization rate is called the overall capitalization rate.

The formula for Overall Capitalization Rate is:

Overall Capitalization Rate = Net Operating Income
÷ Value of Property

In the above example, the acquisition price of the property is $1,150,000, which is also the value. The Gross Operating Income of the property is $177,000, the Operating Expenses are $82,000, so the Net Operating Income is $95,000. We get the worksheet below:

Cash Flow Analysis – Operating Data

Property Name: 123 Main Street, Main City

Down Payment: $500,000

+ Costs of Acquisition: $50,000

= Investment at Purchase: $550,000   + Debt: $600,000   = Acquisition Price $1,150,000

	Mortgage Data	Beginning Balance	Term / Amortization	Number of payments per year	Interest Rate	Payment	Annual Debt Service	Remarks
1.	1st Mortgage	$600,000	5 YR/25 YR	12	5%	$3,489.63	$41,875.56	
2.	2nd Mortgage							

Ownership Analysis of Property Income   **Taxable Income**

		Year 1	Year 2	Year 3	Year 4	Year 5
3	Potential Rental Income	$185,000				
4	Minus: Vacancy & Credit Losses:	$9,250				
5	Equals: Effective Rental Income	$175,750				
6	Plus: Other Income	$1,250				
7	Equals: Gross Operating Income	$177,000				
8	Minus: Operating Expenses	$82,000				
9	Equals: Net Operating Income	$95,000				
10	Minus: Non-operating Expense					
11	Minus: Interest - 1st Mortgage					
12	Minus: Interest - 2nd Mortgage					
13	Minus: Amortization of Loan Fees					
14	Minus: Others					
15	Minus: Others					
16	Equals: Subtotal Taxable Income Before Depreciation					
17	Minus: Allowable Depreciation					
18	Equals: Real Estate Taxable Income					
19	Times: Marginal Tax Rate					
20	Equals: Tax Liability on Real Estate Operations					

Cash Flows

21	Net Operating Income					
22	Minus: Annual Debt Service					
23	Equals: Cash Flow Before Taxes					
24	Minus: Tax Liability (Line 20)					
25	**Equals Cash Flows After Tax**					

Overall Capitalization Rate = $95,000 ÷ $1,150,000

= 0.0826 (8.26%)

When more similar properties are analyzed using this Overall Capitalization Rate formula in the same region, a market capitalization rate can be established using the mean of all capitalization rates obtained.

Suppose the average capitalization rate is 0.08 (8%) after calculating all the recently sold investment properties near the property in the above example. There is another investment property for sale which generates $560,000 net income. Using the formula of Overall Capitalization rate,

Overall Capitalization Rate = Net Operating Income
÷ Value of Property

We have,

Value of Property = Net Operating Income
÷ Overall Capitalization Rate

Therefore, for the new investment property, we have:

Value of Property = Net Operating Income
÷ Overall Capitalization Rate

= $560,000 ÷ 0.08

= $7,000,000

The simple notation of the formula is V = I ÷ R, where V is the value or price, I is the net income generated by the property, and R is the Overall Capitalization Rate.

We can use the above formula and the average capitalization rate of 8% to estimate the value of all other investment properties in the same region.

Payback Period

The Payback Period is used to determine the number of years required for cumulative cash flow before-tax to equal initial investment. That is, it measures the time that an investor needs recoup the initial investment. Its formula is simple:

Payback Period = Cash Investment ÷
Cash Flow Before Taxes

Using the same example above, we can calculate the Net Operating Income of that property is $177,000 – $82,000, = $95,000, the Cash Flow Before Taxes is $95,000 – $41,875.56, = $53,124.44.

Payback Period = $550,000 ÷ $53,124.44

= 10.35 (years)

Therefore, the buyer of that property will have to wait 10.35 years before the initial investment is recouped. However, there is an assumption that no tax is payable for the income earned as the calculation is based on before-tax income, although some investors will use the after-tax Payback Period. Below is the revised worksheet.

Cash Flow Analysis – Operating Data

Property Name: 123 Main Street, Main City

Down Payment: $500,000

+ Costs of Acquisition: $50,000

= Investment at Purchase: $550,000   + Debt: $600,000   = Acquisition Price $1,150,000

	Mortgage Data	Beginning Balance	Term / Amortization	Number of payments per year	Interest Rate	Payment	Annual Debt Service	Remarks
1.	1st Mortgage	$600,000	5 YR/25 YR	12	5%	$3,489.63	$41,875.56	
2.	2nd Mortgage							

Ownership Analysis of Property Income   **Taxable Income**

		Year 1	Year 2	Year 3	Year 4	Year 5
3	Potential Rental Income	$185,000				
4	Minus: Vacancy & Credit Losses:	$9,250				
5	Equals: Effective Rental Income	$175,750				
6	Plus: Other Income	$1,250				
7	Equals: Gross Operating Income	$177,000				
8	Minus: Operating Expenses	$82,000				
9	Equals: Net Operating Income	$95,000				
10	Minus: Non-operating Expense					
11	Minus: Interest - 1st Mortgage	$29,412.02				
12	Minus: Interest - 2nd Mortgage					
13	Minus: Amortization of Loan Fees					
14	Minus: Others					
15	Minus: Others					
16	Equals: Subtotal Taxable Income Before Depreciation					
17	Minus: Allowable Depreciation					
18	Equals: Real Estate Taxable Income	$65,587.98				
19	Times: Marginal Tax Rate					
20	Equals: Tax Liability on Real Estate Operations					

Cash Flows

21	Net Operating Income	$95,000.00				
22	Minus: Annual Debt Service	$41,875.56				
23	Equals: Cash Flow Before Taxes	$53,124.44				
24	Minus: Tax Liability (Line 20)					
25	**Equals Cash Flows After Tax**					

Cash-on-Cash

Cash-on-Cash is a simple ratio of annual before-tax cash flow to the total amount of cash invested, usually expressed as a percentage. It is used to evaluate the cash flow before taxes in a single year by comparing it to the capital

46

invested in the property. It is, actually, the reverse of the Payback Period. The formula of Cash-on-Cash is:

Cash-on-Cash = Cash Flow Before Taxes ÷ Cash Investment

Using the above example, the Cash Flow Before Taxes is $53,124.44, and the cash invested is $550,000.

$$Cash\text{-}on\text{-}Cash = \$53,124.44 \div \$550,000$$

$$= 0.0966$$

$$= 9.66\%$$

Even for the same property, the Cash-on-Cash is not a fixed ratio. If more cash is invested as the down payment, the Cash-on-Cash will change, and the extra cash investment may get a rate of return less than or more than 9.66%, depends on the mortgage rate. We will discuss it in the following chapter.

5. Compounding and Discounting

In order to study more valuation methods, it is necessary to understand the compounding and discounting concepts. Compounding also applies to mortgage calculations.

Compound Interest

There are two ways of calculating interest, simple interest and compound interest. Investors rarely buy simple interest products; they prefer compound interest products because of the higher return. Simple interest is the interest payable for a fixed amount for a specified period at a given rate.

Suppose we put $10,000 in an interest-bearing account that offers an interest rate of 10% per annum. The interest earned at the end of the first year will be $1,000. If we take the interest out of the account right after receiving it, the principal in the account that can earn interest will remain at $10,000. Provided that the interest rate does not change, the account will earn $1,000 interest every year. On the other hand, if we close the account after half a year, the interest earned will also be half of the whole amount, which is $500. That is a typical case to show how simple interest works.

However, if we do not withdraw any money from the account and let the accrued interest earn interest the same way as the principal, the calculations will differ from those in the simple interest case. That is called compound interest. The amount in the account in the first three years are calculated as follows:

Original Principal = $10,000   Interest Rate = 10%

Total amount = Principal + Interest Earned

After the first year: $10,000 + $1,000 = $11,000

After the second year: $11,000 + $1,100 = $12,100

After the third year: $12,100 + $1,210 = $13,310

If we compare this compound interest case with the simple interest case, there is $310 more in the compound interest case after three years. It seems that the difference is not much, but the power of compounding will become more and more significant when the time invested is longer and longer.

After the fourth year: $13,310 + $1,331 = $14,641

After the fifth year: $14,641 + $1,464 = $16,105

After the sixth year: $16,105 + $1,611 = $17,716

After the seven year: $17,716 + $1,771 = $19,487

After seven years, the money in the compound interest account will almost be doubled (195%). After 25 years, it will be ten times the original amount (1,083%). The simple interest case has only 170% and 350% of the original amount after seven and 25 years respectively.

Compound Interest

The formula underlying compounding interest calculation is:

$$T = P (1 + i/n)^N,$$

where: T = Total Compounded Amount

P = Principal (Original) Amount

i = Interest Rate Per Year

n = Number of Periods Per Year

N = Total Number of Periods (as an exponent)

When we use the above example, the total amount in the interest-bearing account after 12 years will be:

$$T = \$10{,}000 \times (1 + 0.1)^{12}$$

$$= \$10{,}000 \times 3.1384$$

$$= \$31{,}384$$

Compare it with the simple interest case, after 12 years, the total amount in the account will be

Principal + Interest = $10,000 + $10,000 x 10% x 12

= $22,000

The return in a compound interest account is significantly higher than that in a simple interest account. That is why investors rarely buy simple interest products. Real estate, on average, has an appreciation of a few percent each year which is on top of the cash flow generated by the rental income. That explains why real estate is one of the most welcome investment tools.

Effective Rates

From the example above, we can see that compounding gives a higher return to the investors. Therefore, most lenders will calculate their loans in compound interest. In fact, the more frequently the interest is calculated in a year, the more interest can be generated.

In the above example, if we change the interest calculation from annual to monthly, the total amount in the account after two years will be calculated as:

$T = P (1 + i /n)^N$

$= \$10,000 \times (1 + 0.1/12)^{36}$

= $10,000 x 1.3482

= $13,482

That is, a monthly compounding will yield $13,482, while an annual compounding will generate only $13,310.

In many jurisdictions, the interest rate posted by a financial institution is a yearly rate subject to further compounding within a year, which is called a nominal rate. The rate actually used for calculation after compounding within a year is called an effective rate. In the above example, the posted rate is 10%, and the effective rate is 10.47%. We can use the formula below to find out an effective rate from a nominal rate:

$R = (1 + i/n)^n - 1$,

where: R = Effective Rate

i = Interest Rate Per Year (Nominal Rate)

n = Number of Periods in a Year

Example

A posted rate of 10%, compounded monthly will have an effective rate as follow:

$R = (1 + i/n)^n - 1$

$= (1 + 0.1/12)^{12} - 1$

= 1.1047 − 1

= 0.1047

= 10.47%

If the interest rate is compounded daily, then we have:

$R = (1 + i/n)^n − 1$

$= (1 + 0.1/365)^{365} − 1$

= 1.1052 − 1

= 0.1052

= 10.52%

That is why most credit card companies charge their customers based on a daily interest rate. The more frequently the rate is compounded, the higher the effective rate is.

Nominal Rates

In some jurisdictions, such as Canada, financial institutions cannot compound their interest more than quarterly or semi-annually. In such a case, the financial institutions must adjust their compounded frequency to the same frequency as the payment method, weekly, bi-weekly or monthly. However, the effective rate after compounding cannot be more than the rate after compounding allowed by law.

For example, financial institutions cannot compound their interest more than twice a year in Canada. If their posted rate (known as nominal rate) is 10%, their effective rate (actual rate charged per year) will be:

$$R = (1 + i/n)^n - 1$$

$$= (1 + 0.1/2)^2 - 1$$

$$= 1.1025 - 1$$

$$= 0.1025$$

$$= 10.25\%$$

They have to convert the effective rate of 10.25% to another nominal rate compounded monthly if the mortgage payment is paid monthly, which will give the same effective rate of 10.25%. From the formula we have,

$$0.1025 = (1 + i/12)^{12} - 1$$

$$1.1025 = (1 + i/12)^{12}$$

$$(1.1025)^{1/12} = (1 + i/12)$$

$$1.008165 = 1 + i/12$$

$$0.008165 = i/12$$

$$i = 0.008165 \times 12$$

$$= 0.09798$$

$$= 9.798\%$$

Therefore, a nominal rate of 9.798% compounded monthly and a nominal rate of 10% compounded semi-annually will give the same effective rate of 10.25% per year. When a financial institution in Canada calculates their mortgage payments for a posted rate of 10%, they will use 9.798% to calculate the interest for clients who want to pay their mortgage payments monthly.

Converting the rates is a difficult task for some people. Fortunately, we have online mortgage calculators that will do the works for us. We have to select the appropriate mortgage calculator[1] as various rules apply to the calculations in different jurisdictions.

Mortgage Basics

A mortgage is simply a loan used by a property owner to raise funds while putting a lien on the property being mortgaged and typically registered in the land registration office. Before calculating how much of a mortgage you can arrange, we have to know some basic terms of a mortgage.

---

[1] Such as https://itools-ioutils.fcac-acfc.gc.ca/MC-CH/MCCalc-CHCalc-eng.aspx

Amortization Period

The time frame that a borrower will have to pay off a mortgage is called the amortization period. The most common amortization period for mortgages is 25 years, but it can be shorter or longer. The longer the amortization period, the more interest you have to pay in total. On the other hand, the shorter the amortization period, the higher the mortgage payments you have to make.

Interest Rate

Interest rate (or the mortgage rate) is the percentage that a lender charges as interest on the amount of money borrowed. Usually, the mortgage rate is fixed within the term, but some financial institutions provide variable rates that float with the prime rate. In commercial mortgages, it is common to have more than one mortgage. The second mortgage usually has an interest rate significantly higher than the first mortgage rate as it has a higher risk. If you need a third mortgage, its rate will be higher than the second mortgage.

Term

A term is a period that a lender guarantees your mortgage, generally from half a year to seven years. That is, the lender is committed to lending you the money for the term and cannot ask for full repayment unless you are in default of the periodic payments. When we say the term, we are also talking about the length of time the interest rate can be fixed. A term can be from six months to five years or even longer.

Rates for shorter terms are usually lower than those for longer terms. For example, when a one-year closed mortgage's interest rate is 5%, the interest rate of a five-year closed mortgage can be 7% or higher.

Open/Closed Mortgage

A term can be open or closed. An open mortgage allows you to pay back the loan for any amount at any time, while a closed mortgage requires you to remain with that lender for the same terms and conditions, or you will be penalized. Interest rates for an open mortgage are higher than for a closed mortgage for the same length of time. Lenders will seldom provide an open mortgage to run for over one year.

Prepayment Option

Advance payment made to the lender under a mortgage agreement can be full or partial payment of the mortgage balance, separate and apart from regular payments. In many jurisdictions, the option of prepayment is a privilege offered by some lenders; it is not a right under the mortgage law.

Renewal Option

A renewal option is essential in a mortgage. Like the prepayment option above, a renewal option is a privilege but not a right. The mortgage law will not stipulate a mortgage must be renewable. A mortgage without a renewal option is risky as once the mortgage matures, the owner will have to pay off the loan in full. In other words, the owner must be able to get another mortgage before the current mortgage expires. Otherwise, the lender can foreclose the property.

Payment option

Many lenders offer payment schedules other than the standard monthly payments. For example, you can pay the mortgage by bi-weekly payments instead of monthly payments. A bi-weekly payment can dramatically shorten your amortization period, say from thirty years to approximately twenty-three years.

Loan Ratio (Loan to Value Ratio or LTV ratio)

That is the ratio of the principal amount of a mortgage (a loan) to the lending value (the appraised value or the purchase price, whichever is less) of the property. A conventional mortgage of residential properties has a maximum LTV ratio of 80%, but lenders typically cap their commercial mortgage LTV ratio at 65%. If an investor needs a commercial mortgage of more than 65% of its value, they will have to apply for a second and even a third mortgage.

Assumption

You can assume the seller's existing mortgage provided that the seller's lender agrees. When buyers assume a mortgage, they take over the mortgage balance and become responsible for the payments, terms, and money owed. By assuming the seller's existing mortgage, the buyers may save appraisal fees, some legal costs, and survey costs. It is particularly good for the buyer if the existing mortgage interest rate is lower than the current rates, although some sellers will ask for a higher price as a trade-off. The advantage to the seller may be a savings of any payout penalty or interest differential that may apply if the seller has to discharge the mortgage before its maturity.

Seller-take-back Mortgage

A seller-take-back mortgage is simply a mortgage offered by a seller, in which the seller acts as the lender. A seller-take-back mortgage is more flexible than the bank's mortgage and is an excellent tool to attract buyers. A renewal option should always be included in the mortgage agreement to protect the buyer.

Interest-only Mortgage

An interest-only mortgage is actually a loan, the borrower pays only the interest on the mortgage amount, and no reduction of principal will be credited during the term. It is also known as a flat-payment mortgage. Interest-only mortgages are not allowed in some jurisdictions. All the mortgage terms may affect the returns of a real estate investment, including the yearly cash flow and the sale proceeds. Investors apply different situations to analyze the investment returns before committing to the mortgage terms and purchasing a property.

Discounting

Discounting is the reverse possess of compounding. In the example above, it takes three years to get $13,310 by depositing $10,000 into an interest-bearing account that gives 10% interest a year, compounded for three years. One of the most common questions for discounting is:

If we will get $13,310 three years later, and the interest rate is 10% per annum, how much money do we have to put into the interest-bearing account now?

The interest rate used in discounting is called the discount rate, as it is used to discount a future value to the value at present (the present value). Therefore, the above question is more commonly written as:

If the value three years later is $13,310, and the discount rate is 10% per annum, what is the present value (what is the present value of $13,310 to be received three years from now)?

Most real estate investment decisions are based on the anticipation of future cash flows; the present value of those cash flows is crucial to value estimates and property comparisons. We have to use discounting method for different types of calculations to compare the properties. Another commonly asked question in real estate using discounting is:

What is the present value of a series of future rental incomes?

As there may be vacancies in the building, bad debt from the tenants and escalation rents within a lease term, the future rental incomes received by the owner will not be equal payments. A financial calculator may not be able to handle such calculations; sophisticated software will usually be used to analyze rental incomes.

Time Value of Money

Compounding and discounting are related to the concepts of the time value of money. In the concept of the time value of money, the money you now receive (the present value) is worth more than the same amount in the future (the future value) because of the potential earning capacity if the money is invested today.

In time value of money calculations, we will have to deal with the following numbers:

1. The Number of Periods in one year (P/YR)
2. The Present Value (PV)
3. The Interest Rate (I)
4. The Total Number of Periods for compounding (N)
5. The Periodic Payments within the period (PMT)
6. The Future Value (FV)

We need to know five of the above numbers to find the sixth one using a financial calculator or an app. The time value of money is a necessary consideration for investments. Its calculations involve the Six Functions of a Dollar. The six functions are:

1. Future Value
2. Present Value
3. Future Value of an Annuity
4. Present Value of an Annuity
5. Amortization of Future Value
6. Amortization of Present Value

Uses

For the function of Future Value, it is often used to project the value of an investment. Suppose we pay an amount for an investment (PV), it earns a return rate (I) per period (P/YR = number of periods per year). The investment runs for a number of periods (N); there is no additional investment and no money withdrawn during the period (PMT = 0). We look for the return on investment (FV).

For the function of Present Value, it is often used to determine the value of an investment. Suppose an investment will provide an amount as the return of investment (FV), after a number of periods (N), a discount rate (I) per period (P/YR = number of periods per year) is used, there is no additional investment and no money withdrawn during the period (PMT =

0). We look for the present value (PV) of the investment, which is the estimated value.

For the function of the Future Value of an Annuity, it is often used to project savings. Suppose there is no initial investment (PV = 0) but a periodic equal saving (PMT) to an interest-bearing account. The account earns an interest rate (I) per year (P/YR = 1), and money will be saved continuously for a number of years (N). We look for the total money saved plus interest (FV) in the saving account after that period.

For the function of the Present Value of an Annuity, it is often used to calculate the insurance annuity. Suppose a client wants to secure a fixed yearly income (PMT) for some years (N), the insurance company uses an interest rate (I) per year (P/YR = 1) to calculate its return, the annuity expires with no residue value (FV = 0) after that. We look for the amount that the client has to pay (PV) for such an annuity.

For the function of Amortization of Future Value, it is often used to calculate the sinking fund amount. Suppose a building needs an amount of money (FV) to replace its shingles after a number of periods (N). Currently, there is no reserve fund for the replacement (PV = 0), and money is being contributed periodically, and it earns an interest rate (I) per period (P/YR = number of periods per year). We look for the money to be contributed in each period (PMT).

For the function of Amortization of Present Value, it is often used to establish loan payment amount. Suppose a borrower gets a loan (PV) with a fixed periodic (P/YR = number of periods per year) interest rate (I). The loan will be amortized over a number of periods (N) so that the balance (FV) will be zero at the end. We look for the periodic payment (PMT) that the borrower has to pay.

All the above six functions are finding the value of PV, FV, or PMT. They are all about the amount of money because it is the Six Functions of a Dollar. In investment analysis, it is common to find out the number of periods (N), as investors are interested to know how long it will take for them to make money, say double of their initial investment. In real estate analysis, we will also try to figure out the I (rate of return) as it is an indicator of the quality of the investments. More complicated calculations and rates, such as IRR, MIRR and FMRR, will be discussed in the following chapters.

Reserve Fund

The time value of money is an essential tool in real estate investment. While a financial calculator can do the job, there are free online apps[2] for easier operations. Spreadsheet and financial software also provide the function of calculating the time value of money.

For real estate investment analysis and property management, calculating the reserve fund contribution

---

[2] Such as https://www.fncalculator.com/financialcalculator?type=tvmCalculator

required to maintain a building is one of the most critical tasks. It is also vital for property managers to calculate the monthly management fees, including condominium fees. Part of the monthly fees will be contributed to the reserve fund to maintain the building.

Example

Question

The property manager of a new condominium building believes that the roof and other major components will have to be replaced in 20 years. The estimated costs of the replacements are $3,000,000, valued at 20 years later. The manager will put the money received in a reserve fund bank account, and the account will earn 3% interest per month. If there are 200 units in the building and each unit owner shares the same costs, how much money will have to be paid by each owner towards the monthly condominium fee to replace the major component 20 years later?

Solution

The financial calculator should be set in the "Begin" mode, as the owners make payments at the beginning of each month. With the background information, we have:

P/YR = 12 (payments are made each month)

N = 240 (months)

PV = 0

I = 3%

FV = $3,000,000

and we look for the value of PMT

The PMT is –$9,115.14 (it is a negative value as the owners pay it out), and there are 200 owners, so each owner will have to pay $45.58 on top of the monthly maintenance fee towards condominium fees.

6. Cash Flow Analysis

The financial analysis of an investment property starts with its Cash Flow Analysis worksheet that we have discussed in Chapter 4.

Cash Flow Analysis – Operating Data

Property Name: _____

Down Payment: _____

+ Costs of Acquisition: _____

= Investment at Purchase: _____ + Debt: _____ = Acquisition Price _____

	Mortgage Data	Beginning Balance	Term / Amortization	Number of payments per year	Interest Rate	Payment	Annual Debt Service	Remarks
1.	1st Mortgage							
2.	2nd Mortgage							

Ownership Analysis of Property Income   **Taxable Income**

		Year 1	Year 2	Year 3	Year 4	Year 5
3	Potential Rental Income					
4	Minus: Vacancy & Credit Losses:					
5	Equals: Effective Rental Income					
6	Plus: Other Income					
7	Equals: Gross Operating Income					
8	Minus: Operating Expenses					
9	Equals: Net Operating Income (NOI)					
10	Minus: Non-operating Expense					
11	Minus: Interest - 1st Mortgage					
12	Minus: Interest - 2nd Mortgage					
13	Minus: Amortization of Loan Fees					
14	Minus: Others					
15	Minus: Others					
16	Equals: Subtotal Taxable Income Before Depreciation					
17	Minus: Allowable Depreciation					
18	Equals: Real Estate Taxable Income					
19	Times: Marginal Tax Rate					
20	Equals: Tax Liability on Real Estate Operations					

Cash Flows

21	Net Operating Income					
22	Minus: Annual Debt Service (ADS)					
23	Equals: Cash Flow Before Taxes					
24	Minus: Tax Liability (Line 20)					
25	**Equals Cash Flows After Tax**					

Cash Flow Analysis Worksheet

The worksheet provides mortgage details, which is essential if the buyer wants to assume any of them. It also provides a summary of cash receipts and cash disbursements before taxes, the net operating income and cash flow before taxes. Usually, the data provided is for five years. It provides a uniform detailed structure for recording the owner's actual income and expenses so that the buyer can quickly analyze them.

Usually, the seller will provide such a worksheet to a buyer, but it is beneficial for the buyers to construct their own version. Buyers should review and confirm each entry on the worksheet, including both rental income and operating expenses. A list will be attached to the worksheet to show the details of all operating expenses. Unless the tenants reimburse all expenses, buyers should ensure that the operating expenses reflect the actual and all necessary expenses to maintain the building.

When examining the worksheet, buyers should pay attention to the following areas:

1. The cost of acquisition
2. The existing mortgage balance and the privileges in the mortgage agreement
3. The potential rental income and the actual income
4. The calculation of projected incomes

5. How the vacancy and credit losses are estimated
6. The source and calculation of extra income
7. The amount of maintenance and repair costs
8. The types of maintenance and repairs
9. The amount of management expense
10. The calculation of projected expenses

Reconstruct the Worksheet

Buyers should review all the numbers on the Cash Flow Analysis worksheet to ensure that they are correct and apply to their own situations. The worksheet can help the buyers forecast possible scenarios based on their own needs after the sale, such as making improvements to the building to bring the rent level up.

Below are some areas that may need changes:

1. The cost of acquisition should be well estimated, including all professional fees and taxes, such as land transfer tax.
2. If the buyers are going to assume the existing mortgage, they should verify the mortgage balance and payment amount, its privileges.
3. The potential rental income may not be the actual income. The potential rental income is the income under the assumption that the property is fully rented at market rents. Many landlords are too optimistic about getting a high market rent.

4. The following few years' incomes may be the actual incomes, but they can also be projected. The escalations of rents should be reasonable.
5. The vacancy and credit losses may not be well reflected or may be underestimated. Different types of properties and different locations have various vacancy rates. In general, residential properties have lower vacancy and credit losses than commercial properties. The vacancy and credit losses can never be zero.
6. The extra income may not be stable and may be overestimated.
7. The maintenance and repair costs may not be the market price as the work may be done by the owner.
8. The existence of maintenance and repairs may not mean that all required works have been done.
9. Management expense is often overlooked or underestimated, especially when it is done by the owner.
10. Expenses are projected for a few years and may not reflect the actual inflation level.

Sometimes, the numbers are all correct, but they may only apply to the seller. For example, the premium for fire insurance of the building is $10,000, and the seller is able to produce a receipt as proof. However, the seller may not tell the buyers that the premium is significantly lower than the market average because the seller owns several investment buildings. The fire insurance of that building is under a blanket insurance policy with other buildings. If a buyer fails to find out such a fact, the increase of fire insurance premium to a standalone building can significantly reduce the return of investment after the sale.

Taxable Income and Cash Flow

The Cash Flow Analysis worksheet has two calculation parts. The first part is to calculate the taxable income and the second part is for the cash flow. We must know the difference and how to interpret the numbers.

Taxable income includes the equity in the property that an investor cannot use, which is the principal portion of the mortgage payment. When the mortgage balance is paid down, the owner has more equity in the real property, but it cannot be used until the property is sold. On the other hand, such money is an income of the owner; therefore, it must be taxed. That is why only the interest portion of the mortgage payment can be deducted from the Net Operating Income in that section.

In the example that we used in Chapter 4, only the interest portion of the mortgage payment ($29,412.02) will be deducted from the Net Operating Income when we calculate the real estate taxable income. However, when we calculate the cash flow before taxes, the whole mortgage payment ($41,875.56) is used as we must pay the entire mortgage payment to the lender, although the principal portion is used to reduce the mortgage balance. That will reduce the cash flow.

Therefore, the taxable income before depreciation will be $65,587.98, while the cash flow before tax is $53,124.44, as shown in the worksheet below.

Cash Flow Analysis – Operating Data

Property Name: 123 Main Street, Main City

Down Payment: $500,000

+ Costs of Acquisition: $50,000

= Investment at Purchase: $550,000   + Debt: $600,000   = Acquisition Price $1,150,000

	Mortgage Data	Beginning Balance	Term / Amortization	Number of payments per year	Interest Rate	Payment	Annual Debt Service	Remarks
1.	1st Mortgage	$600,000	5 YR/25 YR	12	5%	$3,489.63	$41,875.56	
2.	2nd Mortgage							

Ownership Analysis of Property Income   **Taxable Income**

		Year 1	Year 2	Year 3	Year 4	Year 5
3	Potential Rental Income	$185,000				
4	Minus: Vacancy & Credit Losses:	$9,250				
5	Equals: Effective Rental Income	$175,750				
6	Plus: Other Income	$1,250				
7	Equals: Gross Operating Income	$177,000				
8	Minus: Operating Expenses	$82,000				
9	Equals: Net Operating Income	$95,000				
10	Minus: Non-operating Expense					
11	Minus: Interest - 1st Mortgage	$29,412.02				
12	Minus: Interest - 2nd Mortgage					
13	Minus: Amortization of Loan Fees					
14	Minus: Others					
15	Minus: Others					
16	Equals: Subtotal Taxable Income Before Depreciation					
17	Minus: Allowable Depreciation					
18	Equals: Real Estate Taxable Income	$65,587.98				
19	Times: Marginal Tax Rate					
20	Equals: Tax Liability on Real Estate Operations					

Cash Flows

21	Net Operating Income	$95,000.00				
22	Minus: Annual Debt Service	$41,875.56				
23	Equals: Cash Flow Before Taxes	$53,124.44				
24	Minus: Tax Liability (Line 20)					
25	**Equals Cash Flows After Tax**					

In this case, the cash flow before tax amount is less than the cash flow before tax, but it is not always true. The two amounts will be the same if there is no mortgage and no depreciation deducted from the Net Operating Income. Moreover, some Non-operating Expenses, such as finance charges, may reduce the taxable income. More importantly, most investors will apply depreciation to reduce their tax liability.

Depreciation

Depreciation is the decrease of the fair value of an asset, such as the decrease in value of an automobile each year, as it is used and worn. In real estate, it refers to the reduction in the value of the improvements, including buildings.

In accounting, depreciation is a tax sheltering method to reduce or eliminate the taxes due to rental income. Since the land stays forever, it cannot be depreciated. Therefore, the buyer and seller must agree on allocating value on the land and building in their agreement of purchase and sale to comply with the tax law.

In some jurisdictions, depreciation has other names. For example, it is called Capital Cost Allowance (CCA) in Canada. The calculations of depreciation may vary from jurisdiction to jurisdiction. It is a percentage (depreciation rate) of the building value that the owner can use to reduce the rental income. For different types of properties, the depreciation rate and method may not be the same.

Although investors can reduce their taxable income using depreciation, it is just a tax deferral tool in most countries. The total amount claimed by depreciation to reduce the yearly income will become taxable income when the investors sell the property. For example, if an owner claims the depreciation of a property for $20,000 each year continuously for fifteen years and then sells it, the owner will have claimed an accrued $300,000 depreciation. When the owner files the tax return for the year that the property is sold, there will be a $300,000 depreciation recapture and added to the taxable income, although the owner does not receive that $300,000 income.

Therefore, it is better to sell an investment property with depreciation claimed as late as possible. The tax payable in the future because of the depreciation recapture will become neglectable if the period is long enough for the money to depreciate.

It is essential to know that the value in the future is less than its present value. For the same amount of money, the real value at the present time is much more than that in the future. For example, if we put $100 in an interest-bearing account with an annual interest rate of 10% for 100 years, the total amount in that account will be based on this formula:

$$T = P \left(1 + i/n\right)^N$$

$$T = \$100 \times (1 + 0.1)^{100}$$

$$= \$100 \times 13780.61$$

$$= \$1,378,061$$

In other words, $100 at today's value is the same as $1,378,061 after 200 years if it earns an annual interest rate of 10%. By the same token, we say $1,378,061 in 100 years later is the same as $100 now if we use a 10% discounting rate to bring the value back from 100 years later to its present value.

Suppose a property has claimed about $3,000,000 depreciation, and the tax payable due to that depreciation recapture is $1,378,061. Applying the discounting concept and the calculations above, $1,378,061 payable 100 years later will be the same as $100 today with a 10% yearly discount rate. In other words, if the property is sold 100 years after the owner purchased it, the tax payable due to depreciation recapture is neglectable. That is why most investors will hold their investment properties as long as possible and use corporations to hold them, as corporations can last forever but not individuals.

On the other hand, since the depreciation amount claimed will become taxable income when a property is sold, it may not be a good idea to claim depreciation if the owner has no plan to hold the property for an extended period of time.

Suppose an investor sells an investment property after holding it for five years. Each year the investor claims $100,000 as depreciation, so there will be a $500,000 depreciation recapture upon the sale of the property. For five years, the value of that $500,000 will not be depreciated too much. However, when it is added to the investor's taxable income, it may significantly increase the marginal tax rate of the investor, especially if the investor is an individual. Therefore, once investors have claimed depreciation for tax deferral, they should not sell the property within a short period of time.

Interest Rate and Amortization Period

The cash flow before tax that an investor can receive from an investment will be affected by several factors. Does the property has a mortgage? How much is the mortgage rate? What is the length of the amortization period of the mortgage? All these factors, in addition to the depreciation claim, will also affect the resulting taxable income.

When there is no mortgage arranged, the cash flow before tax will be all the net rent received, and the taxable income can only be reduced by depreciation. When there is a mortgage arranged, the cash flow will be reduced by the annual debt service paid to the lender and mortgage interest can be deducted to reduce the taxable income. We can compare the following scenarios.

Depends on the case, sometimes investors will arrange for a mortgage even though they have enough money to purchase the investment property in cash, which is related to the leverage that will be discussed in the next section.

Scenario 1

Cash Flow Analysis – Operating Data

Property Name: 123 Main Street, Main City

Down Payment: $1,100,000

+ Costs of Acquisition: $50,000

= Investment at Purchase: $1,150,000   + Debt: $0   = Acquisition Price $1,150,000

	Mortgage Data	Beginning Balance	Term / Amortization	Number of payments per year	Interest Rate	Payment	Annual Debt Service	Remarks
1.	1st Mortgage							
2.	2nd Mortgage							

Ownership Analysis of Property Income   **Taxable Income**

		Year 1	Year 2	Year 3	Year 4	Year 5
3	Potential Rental Income	$185,000				
4	Minus: Vacancy & Credit Losses:	$9,250				
5	Equals: Effective Rental Income	$175,750				
6	Plus: Other Income	$1,250				
7	Equals: Gross Operating Income	$177,000				
8	Minus: Operating Expenses	$82,000				
9	Equals: Net Operating Income (NOI)	$95,000				
10	Minus: Non-operating Expense					
11	Minus: Interest - 1st Mortgage					
12	Minus: Interest - 2nd Mortgage					
13	Minus: Amortization of Loan Fees					
14	Minus: Others					
15	Minus: Others					
16	Equals: Subtotal Taxable Income Before Depreciation					
17	Minus: Allowable Depreciation	$20,000.00				
18	Equals: Real Estate Taxable Income	$75,000.00				
19	Times: Marginal Tax Rate					
20	Equals: Tax Liability on Real Estate Operations					

	Cash Flows					
21	Net Operating Income	$95,000.00				
22	Minus: Annual Debt Service (ADS)					
23	Equals: Cash Flow Before Taxes	$95,000.00				
24	Minus: Tax Liability (Line 20)					
25	**Equals Cash Flows After Tax**					

The first scenario is that no mortgage is arranged, and the cash flow before tax will be the same as the net operating income before any depreciation is claimed. The taxable income will be reduced by the depreciation claimed. In the example below, the Net Operating Income is $95,000, which is the same as the Cash Flow Before Tax. With an eligible depreciation amount of $20,000, the taxable income is reduced to $75,000.

Scenario 2

Cash Flow Analysis – Operating Data

Property Name: 123 Main Street, Main City

Down Payment: $500,000

+ Costs of Acquisition: $50,000

= Investment at Purchase: $550,000   + Debt: $600,000   = Acquisition Price $1,150,000

	Mortgage Data	Beginning Balance	Term / Amortization	Number of payments per year	Interest Rate	Payment	Annual Debt Service	Remarks
1.	1st Mortgage	$600,000	5 YR/25 YR	12	10%	$5,366.92	$64,403.04	
2.	2nd Mortgage							

Ownership Analysis of Property Income   **Taxable Income**

		Year 1	Year 2	Year 3	Year 4	Year 5
3	Potential Rental Income	$185,000				
4	Minus: Vacancy & Credit Losses:	$9,250				
5	Equals: Effective Rental Income	$175,750				
6	Plus: Other Income	$1,250				
7	Equals: Gross Operating Income	$177,000				
8	Minus: Operating Expenses	$82,000				
9	Equals: Net Operating Income (NOI)	$95,000				
10	Minus: Non-operating Expense					
11	Minus: Interest - 1st Mortgage	$58,527.70				
12	Minus: Interest - 2nd Mortgage					
13	Minus: Amortization of Loan Fees					
14	Minus: Others					
15	Minus: Others					
16	Equals: Subtotal Taxable Income Before Depreciation	$36,472.30				
17	Minus: Allowable Depreciation	$20,000.00				
18	Equals: Real Estate Taxable Income	$16,472.30				
19	Times: Marginal Tax Rate					
20	Equals: Tax Liability on Real Estate Operations					

Cash Flows

21	Net Operating Income	$95,000.00				
22	Minus: Annual Debt Service (ADS)	$64,403.04				
23	Equals: Cash Flow Before Taxes	$30,596.96				
24	Minus: Tax Liability (Line 20)					
25	**Equals Cash Flows After Tax**					

When there is a mortgage, it depends on the loan amount; the cash flow before tax can be reduced significantly to zero or even a negative value. A mortgage with an interest rate of 10%, amortized over 25 years, is arranged in the second scenario. Because of that, both the taxable income and cash flow are reduced by around $60,000.

Scenario 3

Cash Flow Analysis – Operating Data

Property Name: 123 Main Street, Main City

Down Payment: $500,000

+ Costs of Acquisition: $50,000

= Investment at Purchase: $550,000   + Debt: $600,000   = Acquisition Price $1,150,000

	Mortgage Data	Beginning Balance	Term / Amortization	Number of payments per year	Interest Rate	Payment	Annual Debt Service	Remarks
1.	1st Mortgage	$600,000	5 YR/25 YR	12	16%	$7,914.42	$94,973.03	
2.	2nd Mortgage							

Ownership Analysis of Property Income   **Taxable Income**

		Year 1	Year 2	Year 3	Year 4	Year 5
3	Potential Rental Income	$185,000				
4	Minus: Vacancy & Credit Losses:	$9,250				
5	Equals: Effective Rental Income	$175,750				
6	Plus: Other Income	$1,250				
7	Equals: Gross Operating Income	$177,000				
8	Minus: Operating Expenses	$82,000				
9	Equals: Net Operating Income (NOI)	$95,000				
10	Minus: Non-operating Expense					
11	Minus: Interest - 1st Mortgage	$92,797.94				
12	Minus: Interest - 2nd Mortgage					
13	Minus: Amortization of Loan Fees					
14	Minus: Others					
15	Minus: Others					
16	Equals: Subtotal Taxable Income Before Depreciation	$2,202.06				
17	Minus: Allowable Depreciation	$20,000.00				
18	Equals: Real Estate Taxable Income	$0.00				
19	Times: Marginal Tax Rate					
20	Equals: Tax Liability on Real Estate Operations					

		Cash Flows				
21	Net Operating Income	$95,000.00				
22	Minus: Annual Debt Service (ADS)	$94,973.03				
23	Equals: Cash Flow Before Taxes	$26.97				
24	Minus: Tax Liability (Line 20)					
25	**Equals Cash Flows After Tax**					

When the mortgage rate is increased from 10% to 16%, the annual debt service is increased from $64,403.04 to $94,973.03. In this scenario, the cash flow is almost zero, which is not a healthy level. Any decrease in rental income, such as more vacancy and bad debts, can make the cash flow negative. If the owner does not have other income sources, the mortgage may be in default at any time.

Scenario 4

Cash Flow Analysis – Operating Data

Property Name: 123 Main Street, Main City

Down Payment: $500,000

+ Costs of Acquisition: $50,000

= Investment at Purchase: $550,000   + Debt: $600,000   = Acquisition Price $1,150,000

	Mortgage Data	Beginning Balance	Term / Amortization	Number of payments per year	Interest Rate	Payment	Annual Debt Service	Remarks
1.	1st Mortgage	$600,000	5 YR/8 YR	12	5%	$ 7,581.31	$90,975.72	
2.	2nd Mortgage							

Ownership Analysis of Property Income   **Taxable Income**

		Year 1	Year 2	Year 3	Year 4	Year 5
3	Potential Rental Income	$185,000				
4	Minus: Vacancy & Credit Losses:	$9,250				
5	Equals: Effective Rental Income	$175,750				
6	Plus: Other Income	$1,250				
7	Equals: Gross Operating Income	$177,000				
8	Minus: Operating Expenses	$82,000				
9	Equals: Net Operating Income (NOI)	$95,000				
10	Minus: Non-operating Expense					
11	Minus: Interest - 1st Mortgage	$28,282.90				
12	Minus: Interest - 2nd Mortgage					
13	Minus: Amortization of Loan Fees					
14	Minus: Others					
15	Minus: Others					
16	Equals: Subtotal Taxable Income Before Depreciation	$66,717.10				
17	Minus: Allowable Depreciation	$20,000.00				
18	Equals: Real Estate Taxable Income	$46,717.10				
19	Times: Marginal Tax Rate					
20	Equals: Tax Liability on Real Estate Operations					

		Cash Flows				
21	Net Operating Income	$95,000.00				
22	Minus: Annual Debt Service (ADS)	$90,975.72				
23	Equals: Cash Flow Before Taxes	$4,024.28				
24	Minus: Tax Liability (Line 20)					
25	**Equals Cash Flows After Tax**					

On the other hand, some investors will make the cash flow to the minimum level using a shorter amortization period. The main benefit is, of course, to save interest payments. The mortgage rate of the original scenario of our example is 5%, amortized over 25 years. If we change the amortization period from 25 years to 8 years, the mortgage payment will increase to more than $90,000 a year, and the cash flow will be reduced to four thousand more or less.

The benefit is that more than two-thirds of the mortgage payment is the principal payment, which reduces the balance owing. The taxable income ($46,717.10) is much higher than the cash flow ($4,024.28) since the interest paid to the mortgage (which consequently can be claimed to reduce the taxable income) is less. The investor will have to pay the tax due to this real estate operation using another income source as the cash flow from this real estate investment is not enough to pay the tax. On the other hand, the risk of a shortage of cash flow still exists. In case the vacancy and bad debt increase, the investor may lack the cash flow to pay the mortgage.

Leverage and Yield

Leverage is the process of using borrowed capital for investment. If an investor does not borrow money, there is no leverage. The loan amount that an investor borrow will affect the cash flow of the investment as well as the level of the taxable income. Leverage may increase the investor's return on the investment, but the risk associated is also a consideration.

When there is no mortgage, we use the overall capitalization rate to calculate the return on investment of a property. As discussed in Chapter 4, the formula for Overall Capitalization Rate is:

$$\text{Overall Capitalization Rate} = \text{Net Operating Income} \div \text{Value of Property}$$

In the last example on page 82, the net operating income is $95,000, and the cost of acquisition is $1,150,000; therefore, the overall capitalization rate is $95,000 ÷ $1,150,000 = 0.0826 (8.26%). When a mortgage is arranged at a 5% interest rate and amortized over eight years, the return on investment is calculated differently. The new rate of return is called yield, and its formula is:

$$\text{Yield} = (\text{Net Operating Income} - \text{Mortgage Interest}) \div \text{Investment Capital}$$

In the last example, the net operating income is $95,000, the mortgage interest is $28,282.90, and the investment capital is $550,000 (down payment plus costs of acquisition). Therefore,

$$\begin{aligned} \text{Yield} &= (\$95,000 - \$28,282.90) \div \$550,000 \\ &= \$66,717.10 \div \$550,000 \\ &= 0.1213 \ (12.13\%) \end{aligned}$$

With the arrangement of mortgage, the rate of return is raised from 8.26% to 12.13%.

There are three types of leverage: positive, neutral and negative. Positive leverage occurs when the investment yield exceeds the overall rate of return that would have been realized on a property had no financing been put in place. Neutral leverage is the situation where no increase or decrease in yield occurs as a consequence of leverage. Negative leverage occurs when. The leverage in the above example is a positive one.

When the leverage is positive, an investor may want to borrow more money to increase its return rate further. However, it will also increase the risk of cash flow shortage when the vacancy and bad debt increase, resulting in arrears in mortgage payments. On the other hand, an investor should avoid borrowing money when the leverage is negative. Still, investors will have to borrow money when there is a shortage of capital, even if the leverage is negative, provided that the cash flow is positive and other measures are good.

7. Discounted Cash Flows

The concepts of compounding and discounting are discussed in Chapter 5. A simple example of discounting is illustrated by bringing the future value of a lump sum of money to its present value without doing the detailed calculations. If we want to use a formula to calculate the discounted amount, we will have to reverse the compounding formula. For compounding, we have:

$$T = P (1 + i /n)^N,$$

where: T = Total Compounded Amount
P = Principal (Original) Amount
i = Interest Rate Per Year
n = Number of Periods Per Year
N = Total Number of Periods (as an exponent)

Therefore, the formula of discounted value (present value) will be:

$$PV = FV \div (1 + i /n)^N,$$

where: PV = Present Value
FV = Future Value
i = Discount Rate (Interest Rate Per Period)
n = Number of Periods Per Year
N = Number of Periods (as an exponent)

Discounting Different Cash Flows

When we calculate compounding, the rate is usually called the return rate. When we calculate discounting, the rate is called the discount rate. We may use the formula to calculate the present value of a lump sum money in the future. The cash flows in real estate investments are usually calculated yearly and irregular and can be negative. We have to discount the cash flow of each year to its present value one by one.

The concept of discounting different cash flows from the end of years one to five (EOY 1 to EOY 5) to their present value is illustrated by the diagram below. Each year's cash flow is discounted back to the present value (EOY 0).

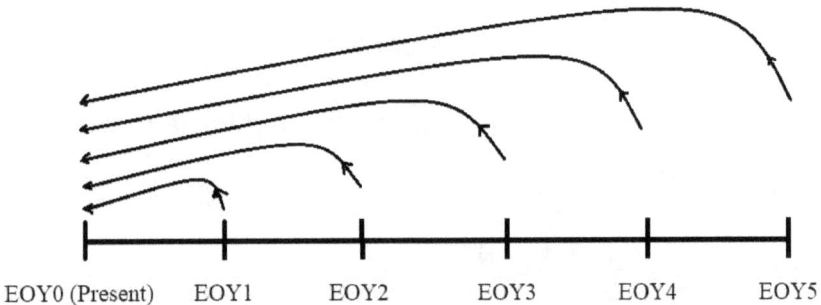

| EOY0 (Present) | EOY1 | EOY2 | EOY3 | EOY4 | EOY5 |

To use a formula for calculation, we have:

$$PV = \sum_{n=1}^{N} \frac{CF_n}{(1+i)^n}$$

where: PV = Present Value

      n   = Number of the Year

      N   = Total number of years

      CF_n = Cash Flow of Year n

      i = Discount Rate

It is a time-consuming task to calculate the present value of a series of cash flows. Besides, it is easy to make mistakes during the computations of the formula. Therefore, we have to rely on a financial calculator to perform the task. There are free online apps[3] to do the calculations too. Real estate investors use sophisticated software to do all investment analysis.

Example

An investment property produces the following incomes: At the end of year 1 (EOY 1) - $25,000, EOY2 - $30,000 and EOY3 - $36,000. As the government bond is 5% and the bank's interest rate is 10%, so the investor uses the two different rates as the discount rates to bring the future cash flows back to their present values.

EOY1 - $25,000
EOY2 - $30,000
EOY3 - $36,000

Total: $91,000

---

[3] Such as https://www.fncalculator.com/financialcalculator?type=irrnpvCalculator

As we just want to discount the future value to its present value, we do not have to know how much money the investor has paid to buy the property. Therefore, we can leave the initial investment (EOY0 or Cash Flow 0) as zero in the calculation. After computing using 5% as the discount rate, the present value of the sum of cash flows is $82,118.56, while the face value is $91,000. When we use 10% as the discount rate, the present value of the cash flows is only $74,567.99.

Comparing Present Values

Since the cash flows generated by a rental property are irregular and sometimes negative, it is easier to evaluate them by discounting them to one present value. We can also compare different cash flows generated by different properties by discounting their cash flows to their present values using the same discount rate.

Example

End of Year	Cash Flow
EOY 1	$60,000
EOY 2	$40,000
EOY 3	$20,000
EOY 4	-$10,000
EOY 5	$30,000
Total	$140,000

The above table shows the cash flows generated by a property in a five-year term. By applying a discount rate of 5%, the present value of the cash flows is $125,979.55.

Another building has similar cash flows as the above property, and an investor wants to compare the two properties. The following table shows the cash flows generated by the other property in the same five-year term.

End of Year	Cash Flow
EOY 1	$55,000
EOY 2	-$20,000
EOY 3	$20,000
EOY 4	$40,000
EOY 5	$45,000
Total	$140,000

By applying the same discount rate of 5%, the present value of these cash flows is $119,683.89. Although the total cash flows of the two properties are the same ($140,000), the present value of the first property is higher. As a result, the first property is better in terms of cash flows.

Net Present Value (NPV)

Investing in real estate needs capital; therefore, we should put the initial capital invested in the property in Year Zero (EOY 0) and denote it as a negative number (negative means giving out and positive means receiving). Once the cash flows of the investment property are discounted to their present value (a positive number), it is added to the initial capital (a negative number), and the sum is called the Net Present Value (NPV), which can be positive or negative.

Example

An investor wants to purchase a building for $1,000,000, which will generate the cash flows shown in the table below.

End of Year	Cash Flow	Sale Proceeds
EOY 0	-$1,000,000	
EOY 1	$55,000	
EOY 2	$60,000	
EOY 3	$60,000	
EOY 4	$70,000	
EOY 5	$75,000	$1,000,000

Assuming that there will be no mortgage arranged and the property will be sold for the same price after five years. We want to calculate the net present value of the cash flows. Using a discount rate of 5%, we have an NPV of $58,512.78 (note: the cash flow of EOY 5 is $1,075,000, which is the sum of the rental cash flow and sale proceeds).

In other words, the cash flows generated by the investment property, using a rate of 5%, have a present value of $1,058,512.78. That is, it is a bargain to buy the property at $1,000,000 as it can generate cash flows that are equivalent to $1,058,512.78 at present.

If we use a higher discount rate of 7%, then the NPV will be –$27,351.13 (a negative value). That is to say; the property is only worth $972,648.87. To compare the different NPVs, a positive NPV indicates a surplus above the discount rate, while a negative NPV means a loss under the discount rate.

Internal Rate of Return (IRR)

By its name, an Internal Rate of Return is the internal measure of the productivity of investment properties. The rate is most commonly stated as an annual rate and only deals with revenue and expenses within the investment project. Nothing external to the investment, such as reinvestment using the cash flows, will be considered.

In a discounted cash flow process, an Internal Rate of Return (IRR) is the discount rate that makes the net present value (NPV) of all cash flows equal to zero. In the above example, we have

End of Year	Cash Flow	Sale Proceeds
EOY 0	-$1,000,000	
EOY 1	$55,000	
EOY 2	$60,000	
EOY 3	$60,000	
EOY 4	$70,000	
EOY 5	$75,000	$1,000,000

If we apply a discount rate of 6.339%, the NPV will be zero. Therefore, the IRR of those cash flows is 6.339%. Mathematically, we have to solve the equation below to find out the IRR.

$$0 = \sum_{n=1}^{N} \frac{CF_n}{(1 + IRR)^n} - CF_0$$

where: n = Number of the Year

N = Total number of years

CF_n = Cash Flow of Year n

CF_0 = Initial Investment (Cash Flow in EOY 0)

IRR = Internal Rate of Return

However, solving such an equation to get the IRR is a complicated task; we can rely on a financial calculator, an online app[4] or software to perform the task.

Example

An investor is interested in a multi-residential building, and the asking price is $2,500,000. The investor plans to buy it in cash, without any mortgage, and hold it for five years. The investor will sell it after five years. The investor wants to analyze this investment using the Internal Rate of Return

---

[4] Such as https://www.fncalculator.com/financialcalculator?type=irrnpvCalculator

(IRR). The projected cash flows and sale proceeds are listed in the table below.

End of Year	Cash Flow	Sale Proceeds
EOY 0	-$2,500,000	
EOY 1	$150,000	
EOY 2	$160,000	
EOY 3	$165,000	
EOY 4	$170,000	
EOY 5	$175,000	$2,600,000

After computation, the IRR is 7.1015%.

In some cases, the internal rate of return may produce ambiguous results or give no answer. For example, the internal rate of return cannot be defined when a series of negative cash flows exceed the initial investment during the holding period. Therefore, other rates are used to measure the performance of investment properties better.

8. MIRR and FMRR

As the IRR is vulnerable to a series of positive and negative sign changes in cash flows or too much negative cash flows, it is modified to provide a more reliable measure. The new rate is called the Modified Internal Rate of Return (MIRR) which uses reinvestment rates to accommodate the negative cash flows.

Modified Internal Rate of Return (MIRR)

MIRR eliminates the issues that IRR has when dealing with multiple sign changes and excludes the possibility of more than one IRR. While IRR assumes that all surplus cash is reinvested at the IRR rate, MIRR uses two different rates. A reinvestment rate is used to compound the positive cash flows, and a finance rate is used to discount the negative cash flows. The formula of MIRR is represented as follows:

$$\text{MIRR} = \sqrt[N]{\frac{\text{FV of all positive cash flows using an reinvestment rate}}{-(\text{PV of all negative cash flows using a finance rate})}} - 1$$

where N is the number of years (or equal periods) at the end of which the cash flows occur, FV is the future value at the end of the last year, and PV is the present value at the beginning of the first year (EOY 0).

<u>Example</u>

An investment property is sold for $500,000 with no mortgage arranged and has even cash flows of $40,000 for the first three years. However, the new owner spent $61,000 in renovation for retrofitting the fire regulations in year one, resulting in a negative cash flow of $21,000 in year one. The property is sold again at the end of year three for $550,000. All the numbers are shown in the table below.

End of Year	Cash Flow	Sale Proceeds
EOY 0	-$500,000	
EOY 1	-$21,000	
EOY 2	$40,000	
EOY 3	$40,000	$550,000

To calculate the MIRR, we must assign a reinvestment rate and a finance rate to the calculations. The rates are usually based on the market rates, such as the banks' term deposit interest rates and their prime rates. If the reinvestment rate is 6% and the finance rate is 5%, the future value and present value of cash flows will be calculated as follows.

1. Future value of positive cash flows:

FV of EOY 2 = $40,000 x 1.06% = $42,400

FV of EOY 3 = $40,000 + $550,000 = $590,000

Total FV = $42,400 + $590,000 = $632,400

2. Present Value of negative cash flows:

PV of EOY 0 = -$500,000

PV pf EOY 1 = -$21,000 ÷ 1.05 = -$20,000

Total PV = -$500,000 + (-$20,000) = -$520,000

3. Calculation of MIRR

$$MIRR = \sqrt[3]{\frac{\$632,400}{-(-\$520,000)}} - 1$$

$$MIRR = \sqrt[3]{\frac{\$632,400}{\$520,000}} - 1$$

$$MIRR = \sqrt[3]{1.2161538} - 1$$

$$MIRR = 1.06741 - 1$$

$$= 0.06741 \ (6.741\%)$$

Again, more complicated calculations will have to rely on simple apps[5] or sophisticated software.

---

[5] Such as https://www.fncalculator.com/financialcalculator?type=mirrCalculator

Financial Management Rate of Return (FMRR)

Like the MIRR, the Financial Management Rate of Return (FMRR) is the internal rate of return that specifies cash flows (inflows and outflows) at two different rates, the reinvestment rate and the finance rate. The difference is that FMRR uses positive cash flows to compensate negative cash flows until they are all positive or have been discounted back to the initial period.

When calculating the FMRR, each negative cash flow is discounted back to the previous period with a positive cash flow at the finance rate. If the previous period also has a negative cash flow, then it is discounted for one more year and so on. The discounted negative cash flow is then added to the positive cash flow. If the result is still a negative cash flow, the process will be repeated until all cash flows are positive or negative cash flows are discounted back to the initial investment.

After discounting the negative cash flows, all positive cash flows have to be compounded to the last period using the reinvestment rate. As a result, only two periods will have non-zero cash flows. The initial period will have a negative amount (initial investment and the possible discounted negative cash flows), and the final period will have all the compounded positive cash flows plus the potential sale proceeds.

The last step is to use the two amounts to calculate the IRR. The resulting IRR using those steps is the FMRR.

Example

A rental apartment building was sold for $3,500,000, and no mortgage was arranged. After holding the property for three years, the owner spent $500,000 in renovation for retrofitting the fire regulations, resulting in a negative cash flow in the fourth year. The property was sold again at the end of year six for $4,000,000.

An analyst wanted to use a reinvestment rate of 5% and a finance rate of 4% to calculate the Financial Management Rate of Return (FMRR). All the cash flows are shown in the table below.

End of Year	Cash Flow	Sale Proceeds
EOY 0	-$3,500,000	
EOY 1	$200,000	
EOY 2	$240,000	
EOY 3	$280,000	
EOY 4	-$156,000	
EOY 5	$400,000	
EOY 6	$450,000	$4,000,000

First Step: Discounting Negative Cash Flows

The only negative cash flow, -$156,000, is in EOY 4. It is discounted to -$150,000 using the finance rate of 4%. This value is added to the cash flow in EOY 3, and the result is

$130,000. Since it is a positive number, no further discounting is needed.

Second Step: Compounding Positive Cash Flows

The cash flow in each year is compounded to EOY 6 using the reinvestment rate of 5%. All the compounded cash flows are then added to the cash flow and sale proceeds in EOY 6. The final results are shown in the table below.

End of Year	Cash Flow
EOY 0	-$3,500,000
EOY 1	$0
EOY 2	$0
EOY 3	$0
EOY 4	$0
EOY 5	$0
EOY 6	$5,567,469

Last Step: Calculating the FMRR

Using the cash flows in the above table, we calculate the IRR to arrive at the FMRR of 8.0434%.

Comparison

Using rates of return to compare the performances of different properties is a valid method only if other measures of those properties are similar. For example, all the buildings and other improvements of the comparing properties should be maintained and retrofitted to the same standard. Otherwise, some of them may need repair or renovation soon, which will significantly reduce the cash flows.

All comparing properties, including vacant lands, should have no environmental risks of any kind. The remediation costs of contaminated properties are very high; sometimes, they can exceed purchase costs. Contaminations may cause other issues such as civil liabilities when they affect the neighbouring properties or

The holding period or the projected income period used to calculate the rates of return of different properties should also be the same. Suppose the holding period or income period of an investment property is longer than the others. In that case, the positive cash flows of other investment properties should be compounded at the reinvestment rate to match the length of the holding period of that investment property.

Sometimes, investors look for a higher return in terms of value but not the rate. Suppose there are two investment properties. The first property is asking for $1,000,000 and offers a 10% return, while the second one is asking for $40,000,000 but offers only a 9% return. The first property has a higher rate of return but produces only $100,000 cash flow a year. Although the second property offers a lower rate of return, it can generate a cash flow of $3,600,000 per year.

An investor who has more than $40,000,000 capital to invest is more likely to buy the second property because the first property is too small to produce enough profit. Unless there are similar properties with the same return rate of 10% as the first property and their total value is $40,000,000; otherwise, an investor will have to accept a 9% return rate for entirely investing $40,000,000 capital.

Suppose there are two investment properties with the same asking price. One property requires a less initial investment because of some reasons, such as the seller offering a take-back second mortgage and the other seller does not. The saved initial capital should be treated as a separate investment and projected to a future value at the end of the holding period using the reinvestment rate. Such an amount should be added to the future value of that investment property for an apple-to-apple comparison.

Case Study

So far, we have discussed a few rates to measure the performance of investment properties, namely, Gross Rent Multiplier, Break-even Ratio, Overall Capitalization Rate, Payback Period, Cash-on-Cash, Present Value, Yield, IRR, MIRR and FMRR. For the same property, different measuring tools may indicate different levels of attractiveness of the investment. Below is a case that we use various tools to apply to it for evaluation.

An investment property is listed for sale at $1,100,000 with a seller-take-back first mortgage of $600,000, bearing interest at a rate of 6% per annum, calculated semi-annually not in advance, amortized over 25 years. The costs of purchase are approximately $50,000. We assume that the property will be sold after five years, and the sale proceeds will be $568,955 after paying all costs and mortgage balance. Details of cash flows are shown in the table below.

Cash Flow Analysis – Operating Data

Property Name: 123 Main Street, Main City

Down Payment: $500,000

+ Costs of Acquisition: $50,000

= Investment at Purchase: $550,000   + Debt: $600,000   = Acquisition Price $1,150,000

	Mortgage Data	Beginning Balance	Term / Amortization	Number of payments per year	Interest Rate	Payment	Annual Debt Service	Remarks
1.	1st Mortgage	$600,000	5 YR/25 YR	12	5%	$3,489.63	$41,875.56	
2.	2nd Mortgage							

Ownership Analysis of Property Income   **Taxable Income**

		Year 1	Year 2	Year 3	Year 4	Year 5
3	Potential Rental Income	$185,000	$192,000	$200,000	$210,000	$222,000
4	Minus: Vacancy & Credit Losses:	$9,250	$9,600	$10,000	$10,500	$11,100
5	Equals: Effective Rental Income	$175,750	$182,400	$190,000	$199,500	$210,900
6	Plus: Other Income	$1,250	$1,250	$1,500	$1,500	$1,750
7	Equals: Gross Operating Income	$177,000	$183,650	$191,500	$201,000	$212,650
8	Minus: Operating Expenses	$82,000	$85,000	$338,000	$90,000	$94,000
9	Equals: Net Operating Income (NOI)	$95,000	$98,650	–$146,500	$111,000	$118,650
10	Minus: Non-operating Expense					
11	Minus: Interest - 1st Mortgage	$29,412	$29,412	$29,412	$29,412	$29,412
12	Minus: Interest - 2nd Mortgage					
13	Minus: Amortization of Loan Fees					
14	Minus: Others					
15	Minus: Others					
16	Equals: Subtotal Taxable Income Before Depreciation	$65,588	$69,238	–$175,912	$81,588	$89,238
17	Minus: Allowable Depreciation	$20,000	$20,000	$20,000	$20,000	$20,000
18	Equals: Real Estate Taxable Income	$45,588	$49,238	$0	$61,588	$69,238
19	Times: Marginal Tax Rate					
20	Equals: Tax Liability on Real Estate Operations					

		Cash Flows				
21	Net Operating Income	$95,000	$98,650	–$146,500	$111,000	$118,650
22	Minus: Annual Debt Service (ADS)	$41,876	$41,876	$41,876	$41,876	$41,876
23	Equals: Cash Flow Before Taxes	$53,124	$56,774	–$188,376	$69,124	$76,774
24	Minus: Tax Liability (Line 20)					
25	**Equals Cash Flows After Tax**					

The buyer will have to retrofit the building to comply with the fire regulations. Renovations will be done in the third year, resulting in a negative cash flow of $188,376.

Gross Rent Multiplier (GRM)

To find out the Gross Rent Multiplier of that property, we recall the formula:

Gross Rent Multiplier = Value ÷ Gross Rent

Therefore,

Gross Rent Multiplier = $1,150,00 ÷ $177,000

= 6.497

The costs of purchase are added to the value. Unlike in Chapter 4, we do not use the Potential Rental Income as the gross rent to calculate the GRM. We use the Gross Operating Income in Year One as it is more accurate after taking vacancy, bad debt and other income into consideration. As discussed in Chapter 4, GRM is not a good measurement of the performance of investment properties.

Break-even Ratio

Similar to calculating the GRM, the data of the first year is used. According to the equation, we have

Break-even Ratio = (Operating Expenses + Debt Service) ÷ Gross Operating Income

Break-even Ratio = ($82,000 + $41,876) ÷ $177,000

Break-even Ratio = $123,876 ÷ $177,000

Break-even Ratio = 0.7 (70%)

The Break-Even Ratio is 70%, which means that the property can still be break-even when its gross operating income reduces by 30% or when the sum of its operating expenses and debt service increase by 42.86%.

Overall Capitalization Rate (OCR)

The formula for Overall Capitalization Rate is:

Overall Capitalization Rate = Net Operating Income ÷ Value of Property

= $95,000 ÷ $1,150,000

= 0.0826 (8.26%)

Again, the costs of purchase are added to the value, and only the data first year is used.

Some sellers will use the average Net Operating Income (NOI) of all projected years to calculate the OCR, as it can give a higher rate to attract buyers. The five years average NOI in this example is $105,360. Therefore,

Average OCR = $105,360 ÷ $1,150,000

= 0.0916 (9.16%)

Payback Period

The formula of the Payback Period is:

Payback Period = Cash Investment ÷
                 Cash Flow Before Taxes

Payback Period = $550,000 ÷ $53,124

= 10.35 (years)

That is, it takes 10.35 years for the buyer to recover the initial capital. However, it is unfair to use only the first-year data to calculate the Payback Period. However, when we use the five-year average Cash Flow Before Taxes,

Payback Period = $550,000 ÷ $13,484

= 40.79 (years)

The average Cash Flow Before Taxes is a low level of $13,484 because the third year cash flow is a negative figure (−$188,376). Should there be no negative cash flow, the Payback Period will be less than ten years if we use the five-year average to calculate it.

Cash-on-Cash

The formula of Cash-on-Cash is:

Cash-on-Cash = Cash Flow Before Taxes ÷ Cash Investment

Cash-on-Cash = $53,124 ÷ $550,000

Cash-on-Cash = $53,124 ÷ $550,000

= 0.0966 (9.66%)

Again, if we use the five-year average Cash Flow Before Taxes, it is only $13,484 due to the negative cash flow. Consequently, the Cash-on-Cash will also be a very low rate.

Present Value

The cash flows of the five years are shown in the table.

Year	Cash Flow	Sale Proceeds
EOY 0	-$550,000	
EOY 1	$53,124	
EOY 2	$56,774	
EOY 3	-$188,376	
EOY 4	$69,124	
EOY 5	$76,774	$568,955

If the discount rate is given as 5%, we can use the below formula to find out the Present Value of the cash flows

$$PV = \sum_{n=1}^{N} \frac{CF_n}{(1+i)^n}$$

where: PV = Present Value

n = Number of the Year

N = Total number of years

CF_n = Cash Flow of Year n

i = Discount Rate

We can also use a financial calculation, online app or software to compute.

$$Present\ Value = \$502,178$$

The initial capital investment (Cash Flow in EOY 0) is not used in computing the Present Value of cash flows. Otherwise, the result will be the Net Present Value. Since the Present Value of all cash flows is less than $550,000 (the initial investment), it means that the return rate is less than the discount rate of 5%.

Yield

The initial investment (with costs) is $550,000. Using the formula, we have

$$Yield = (Net\ Operating\ Income - Mortgage\ Interest)$$
$$\div Investment\ Capital$$

$$Yield = (\$95,000 - \$29,412) \div \$550,000$$

$$= \$65,588 \div \$550,000$$

$$= 0.1193\ (11.93\%)$$

The yield (11.93%) is higher than the OCR (8.26%) because of the low mortgage interest rate (5%). If the mortgage interest rate goes up, the yield will be lowered. The yield will be less than the OCR at a mortgage rate approximately equal to 8.26%. It is because the money borrowed will be required to pay for an interest rate higher than 8.26%, while the investment can only give a return rate of 8.26%.

Internal Rate of Return (IRR)

We will have to rely on a financial calculator, an app or software to calculate the IRR. Remember that an IRR is the rate that makes the Net Present Value zero (the discounted cash flows equal to the initial investment). The cash flows of the property are repeated in the table below:

Year	Cash Flow	Sale Proceeds
EOY 0	-$550,000	
EOY 1	$53,124	
EOY 2	$56,774	
EOY 3	-$188,376	
EOY 4	$69,124	
EOY 5	$76,774	$568,955

After computing, the IRR is 3.0435%

Modified Internal Rate of Return (MIRR)

Before computing the MIRR, we have to select the reinvestment rate and finance rate based on the market. Assuming a reinvestment rate of 5% and a finance rate of 3% are the prevailing rates in the market, we can calculate the MIRR using the formula below, a financial calculator or an app.

$$\text{MIRR} = \sqrt[N]{\frac{\text{FV of all positive cash flows using an reinvestment rate}}{-(\text{PV of all negative cash flows using a finance rate})}} - 1$$

where N is the number of years (or equal periods) at the end of which the cash flows occur, FV is the future value at the end of the last year, and PV is the present value at the beginning of the first year (EOY 0).

After computing, the MIRR is 3.273%. The MIRR is higher than the IRR (3.0435%) because the negative cash flow is discounted using a finance rate of 3%, which is lower than the reinvestment rate of 5%.

Financial Management Rate of Return (FMRR)

Let us use the same rates above to calculate the FMRR, a reinvestment rate of 5% and a finance rate of 3%.

First Step: Discounting the Negative Cash Flow

The only negative cash flow, –$188,376, is in EOY 3. It is discounted to –$182,889 in EOY 2 using the finance rate of 3%. This value is added to the cash flow in EOY 2, and the result is –$126,115. Since it is still a negative number, we discount it again to EOY 1. After the second discounting, the amount is –$122,442,56, and it is added to the cash flow in EOY 1. The result is –$69,318, which is still negative. We further discount it to EOY 0, which is –$67,299. Therefore, the cash flow in EOY 0 (initial investment) becomes –$617,299 instead of –$550,000.

Second Step: Compounding Positive Cash Flows

The positive cash flows in each year are compounded to EOY 5 using the reinvestment rate of 5%. All the compounded cash flows are then added to the cash flow in EOY 5. The final results with the sale proceeds are shown in the table below.

Year	Cash Flow	Sale Proceeds
EOY 0	-$617,299	
EOY 1	$0	
EOY 2	$0	
EOY 3	$0	
EOY 4	$0	
EOY 5	$279,651	$568,955

Last Step: Calculating the FMRR

Using the cash flows in the above table, we calculate the IRR to arrive at the FMRR of 6.5718%.

Conclusion

Real estate investment emphasizes the development potential, legality of use, and financial benefits driven by cash flow, capitalized value and yield comparisons. Although those are vital in the decision-making process, investment analysis must be carried out within the framework of a broader investment strategy. Different methods and strategies are used to meet the needs and goals of the investors.

Real estate investors must conduct their due diligence based on risks, profitabilities, and costs. Investors also need to solve more problems and assess different types of risks: building, business, environmental, financial and market. The investment decision model must consider alternatives in a market with comparable investment opportunities. The above case study provides a glimpse into different investment measuring tools for comparison.

~ The End ~

www.ingramcontent.com/pod-product-compliance
Lightning Source LLC
Chambersburg PA
CBHW070934210326
41520CB00021B/6945